# MACRAME

A Complete Step-by-step Guide Updated & Illustrated for Beginners

(Improve Your Designs With Illustrated Projects and Handmade Patterns for Home and Garden)

**Hipolito Nelson**

Published By **Hipolito Nelson**

Hipolito Nelson

All Rights Reserved

*Macrame: A Complete Step-by-step Guide Updated & Illustrated for Beginners (Improve Your Designs With Illustrated Projects and Handmade Patterns for Home and Garden)*

ISBN 978-1-77485-421-1

All rights reserved. No part of this guide may be reproduced in any form without permission in writing from the publisher except in the case of brief quotations embodied in critical articles or reviews.

Legal & Disclaimer

The information contained in this book is not designed to replace or take the place of any form of medicine or professional medical advice. The information in this book has been provided for educational and entertainment purposes only.

The information contained in this book has been compiled from sources deemed reliable, and it is accurate to the best of the Author's knowledge; however, the Author cannot guarantee its accuracy and validity and cannot be held liable for any errors or omissions. Changes are periodically made to this book. You must consult your doctor or get professional medical advice before using any of the suggested remedies, techniques, or information in this book.

Upon using the information contained in this book, you agree to hold harmless the Author from and against any damages, costs, and expenses, including any legal fees potentially resulting from the application of any of the information provided by this guide. This disclaimer applies to any damages or injury caused by the use and application, whether directly or indirectly, of any advice or information presented, whether for breach of contract, tort, negligence, personal injury, criminal intent, or under any other cause of action.

You agree to accept all risks of using the information presented inside this book. You need to consult a professional medical practitioner in order to ensure you are both able and healthy enough to participate in this program.

# TABLE OF CONTENTS

INTRODUCTION .................................................................. 1

CHAPTER 1: WHAT YOU SHOULD BE ABLE TO DO BEFORE APPROACHING MACRAME ................................................. 4

CHAPTER 2: TIPS FOR MACRAME BEGINNING MACRAME 28

CHAPTER 3: MACRAME CORD ......................................... 46

CHAPTER 4: MACRAME PRACTICE PROJECT ..................... 57

CHAPTER 5: TOOLS AND MATERIALS UTILIZED IN MACRAME MACRAME MATERIALS ................................... 72

CHAPTER 6: IS IT POSSIBLE TO CREATE AN BUSINESS TODAY WITH MACRAME? ................................................ 79

CHAPTER 7: THE TOOLS REQUIRED TO RUN MACRAME. 101

CHAPTER 8: MACRAME KNOT INSTRUCTIONS ............... 111

CHAPTER 9: HOW DO I START THE PROCESS OF STARTING A MACRAME PROJECT .................................................... 116

CHAPTER 10: MACRAME JEWELLERY ............................. 128

CHAPTER 11: HOW TO MAKE A BRACELET .................... 137

CHAPTER 12: HOW TO CREATE COMMON MACRAME KNOTS AND PATTERNS .................................................. 148

**CHAPTER 13: MACRAME PROJECTS** .............................. **156**

**CONCLUSION** ................................................................. **177**

# Introduction

The ancient art of knot-tying to an assortment of patterns Macrame makes a variety of exquisite designs and jewellery which we can get everyday activities. The 20th century saw the macrame was popular during the 1970s. However, it's returning to the new millennium.

Perhaps macrame is becoming well-known because it is easy to understand for all to. When you are studying and practicing macrame knots and techniques and techniques, you will be able to tackle the more challenging and exciting tasks.

Macrame is an amazing work of art to master as it's an effective method of wrist and palm exercises. When you put them in the movements involved in the knots that you tie with macrame your ligaments are kept smooth and powerful.

Macrame is also great for comfort and relaxation after a long day. After wrapping a few knots, you'll begin to relax and be at peace, and this gives satisfaction when you look at the end result of your endeavor.

Are you excited about beginning to learn about macrame?

We'll give you all the necessary information you require to begin your first macrame task. Each chapter will guide you through the macrame procedure from beginning to end. The information you will find in this book:

History of Macrame.

* What is the most popular way to use macrame and the reasons.

* The various forms of cord and which one is best suited for the job.

* How can you figure out how much cording a contractor requires

* How can you ensure that the job is trustworthy and reliable

What are the equipment and resources are you required to launch?

"Basic nodes. Basic nodes

* Knotting complicated. Knotting complex.

* How do I combine macrame and beading?

Tips to begin an online business.

# Chapter 1: What You Should Be Able To Do Before Approaching Macrame

Macrame Materials

MAcrame stylists employ various types of materials. Materials can be classified into two main ways:

Natural Materials

The properties of natural materials differ from synthetic materials and knowing their characteristics will assist you in making the best use of the materials. Natural cord materials available are hemp, jute cotton, leather flax, and silk. There are also fibers made of natural fibers. Fibers made from natural materials are derived by animals and plants.

Synthetic Materials

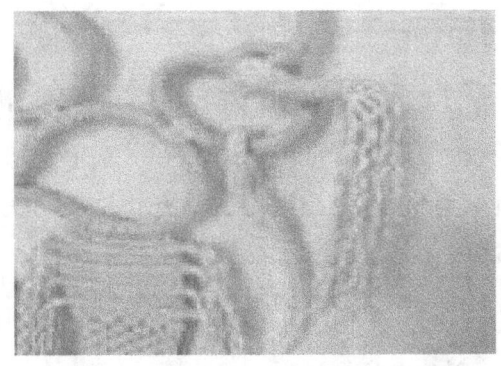

As natural substances synthetic materials are also employed in macrame projects. The synthetic fibers are created by chemical processes. The most popular are nylon beads, the satin cord, olefin as well as parachute cord.

Jewelry Tools

It's a simple set of three tools in order to turn knots or braids into jewelry. The purchase of high-end, quality tools are always worth it because they will allow you to complete tasks swiftly and efficiently. However, do not use mini-tools since they will cause your hands to be uncomfortable when used for prolonged time.

## Wire Cutters

Use side cutters or, ideally, flush-cutters, that cut the headpins or wire to an unidirectional end. Be aware of cutting into the job, or to turn off from the back using the cut side that is flat.

## Round-Nose Pliers

These pliers can be utilized to make headpins or wire loops. Jaws are cone-shaped therefore you can adjust the size of the loop by using tiny loops towards on the high end of jaws, and for larger loops at the bottom. It is common to use the same distance downwards to create loops that are similar dimensions. They can be utilized to control wires and headpins, or for opening and closing the jump rings. It is recommended to search for relatively smooth surfaces inside of the jaws. Pinholes bought found at your local hardware store are not suitable due to their size. In addition to being too large they also contain deep grip serrations that could cause damage to the metal. Blunt-end pliers are a great tool for the workhorses, however the pliers snipped-nose (chain-nose) equipped with tapered jaws permit you to be closer. Tools that are specialized but not necessary This kit can help you finish your jewelry professionally and should be considered a purchase in it if you are able to.

Bent-Nose Pinions

They're basically snipe-nose-style gears that have an right-angle bend in the jaws. This allows users to maneuver into difficult position and hold wires or headpins if needed at a more relaxed angle.

Nylon-Jaw Pliers

They have a softer material that is used to cover the jaws of the metal to avoid the deterioration of wires that are softer and the resulting. They can be found in round-nose and flat-nose.

Crimp Pliers

Three sizes are available-micro, macro, and medium. These instruments are primarily used to seal crimps securely around threads of beading.

The pliers are matched to the wire's thickness as well as the dimensions of the crimp.

Split-Ring Pinions

With a specially designed edge for splitting-ring openings These will definitely assist to avoid broken nails!

Awl

Awls are useful for moving cords and braids around metal and making them easier to move.

Warp Posts

Attach the clamp to the edge of the work area and set a specific distance to allow winding longer cord lengths.

Certain Essentials

These tools can be located in your toolbox. They are useful for braiding and knotting.

Scissors

Use two to three different kinds of scissors solely to cut cords and threads, and don't use scissors for cutting paper as cutting paper can damage the blades quite easily. Large scissors are ideal to cut the length of cords and threads. smaller scissors with sharp spots can be used for smooth cutting of the ends.

Needles

Any needle can create knots, finishing braids or thread beads simpler.

* Sewing needles The set of sew needles in various sizes allows you to stitch through braids or tie ends up after wrapping. Sharps are tiny but are robust and can be used to thread tiny seed beads into stronger strings. The eyes of embroidery needles are longer to make threading easier.

* Tapestry needles: They are made with a sharp tip and a big eye, and can be used for stringing larger beads on cords or to manipulate knots to secure them. Fine beading needles can be used to join seed beads and other beads to the braids , or to cover joints. They are ideal to use for seed beads of size 11, as well as sizes 12 and 13 to accommodate size 15 seed beads, using a sizes 10 needle. Maintain a stock of good quality, since the smaller needles are more likely to break and bend in particular.

Twisted wire needles: By connecting the fine wire to the jaws of round-nosepliers and pulling the tails to join to create your own requirements. You can also get them purchased in a variety of sizes to connect beads to thread or a cord, or pull loops or cords in order to tidy ends to braid them.

"Big eye" needles long two-pointed needles can be used to string beads onto multiple fine threads, however, avoid pulling cords into tight spaces due to the two rods are separated from the needle from the soldered end.

* Pins for dressmaker's pins can be used to mark braids at a particular length as well as spacing beads or other embellishments and for arranging the threads that are wrapped.

Map Pins

These pins that are short and have ball ends are great for using macrame to shield the threads and cords. Connect it to corkboards or a the foam core frame.

## Adhesives

to tie threads and cords as well as render jewelry and accessories. Select the most suitable adhesive that matches the material that you adhere to, and make sure you allow for at least 24 hours. The glues such as G-S Hypo Cement and E6000 are specially designed for use in jewelry. The glue is formed but remains flexible, which makes it less likely to break and break over time. The G-S Hypo Cement comes with the perfect nozzle to apply a small amount to achieve a smooth surface and then using an application stick for the glue.

## Superglue

Instant glues are helpful because the substance should not be removed from the surface until the glue has set. More likely to be able to run the gel-based version, as it's simpler to maintain consistency by adding a tiny amount. Be careful because these glues made of Cyanoacrylate can bind skin.

Epoxy Resin

Two-part adhesives are ideal for attaching cords to metal objects. Wipe surfaces clean using nail polish remover prior to adhering the adhesive in order to get rid of dirt-stained fingerprints. The 5-minute epoxy resin reduces drying time. When it is used, one that has dried clear is less likely to be obvious.

Macrame Boards

Macrame projects should be fixed to a work surface when you are working, typically using masking tape and/or T pins. This allows you to manage your cords and also helps keep the knots secured and aligned. At your local bead and craft shop, or online retailers, specially-designed macrame boards are readily available and are suitable for all kinds of tasks. They typically measure 12" x 18 30cm (30cm 46cm) and are made from fiberboard. The majority of macrame boards include a grid on their surface, and rulers on the sides. They are able to be removed however, I prefer to keep them in place , either shrink-wrapped or sealed, since I believe they are very useful guidebooks when working. Many also have the basic macrame knots to help with instruction.

Pins and tape Pins

With pins, your work is secured to the macrame board to ensure it isn't able to move while you work. Pins also work when you incorporate different knot sequences as well as other design elements in your projects , to help keep the strands secure.

The most commonly used macrame option is t-pins. They're long and shape that allows them to remove and insert repeatedly. This also allows you to make use of ball-end pins to sew, however they're not as sturdy as T-pins. Stop replacing the push pins and thumbtacks that are both too short.

It also makes use of masking tape to secure material to the surface. If you're working with a delicate surface, it could be a suitable replacement for T-pins. However, it's typically employed to secure "filler cords"--or cords to connect your work cords to while making knots that are square and twisting. (On the next page you'll find more information details about them). I like using the blue masking tape since it's simpler to take off and move around while working than the typical masking press. Do not remove duct tape, packaging tape as well as any similar transparent tapes; they're all sticky and could damage your cords as well as surfaces, and they're difficult to get rid of from all over.

Cords

If you are able to tie knots, you'll likely be able to macrame using it. Waxed linen as well as waxed hemp are among the most commonly used fibers to work with. They are available in a broad variety of thicknesses and colors. The wax coating that is applied to these cords makes them extremely easy to maintain the knot. The knots you tie and the knot patterns will be clearly described. Cords are available from craft and bead shops, or you can find the cords online.

Another well-known macrame material is rattail. It is a satin cord which comes in a rainbow of colors and has at minimum three different thicknesses. The 1970s saw rattail becoming a popular choice. became very popular, but has never ever went out of fashion for artists who prefer to incorporate Chinese Knots or Celtic Knots into their work. It is a bit slippery and if it is not secured knots that are tied into the rattail may loosen. The results are so stunning that it is worth it to use this product.

Wire

Wire is a difficult material to work with, but when you are skilled at the art it can result in distinctive pieces of jewellery. The principle of metal is not to be bent repeatedly. It is weak, and the repetitive bending of the wire to break and work-hardened. When you twist it in a circular motion, repeatedly eventually, it will crack. The heavier wire is also less able to bend without a significant quantity of work. Most metal macrame is created of thinner gauge wire making it easier to work with. When it's in motion, it will always become stiffer however, the smaller the bend the more flexible it will be.

If you've not experienced wire in the past, then you may need to become more familiar with it by first using the less expensive metal wire. There are many types of wire to pick from, including copper, brass and art wire that come in a range of shades. The majority of these tubes are also referred to as gauges, come in various sizes. Because of the size, the thinner the gauge number more thick, the stronger the wire will be difficult to bend.

Examining the Knots

When you are ready to start learning to Macrame make sure you have your tools and become familiar with the standard Macrame specifications you'll have to master.

Substances and Supplies

Here's what you're going to need to learn and then figure on how to make your own Macrame knots:

* Macrame cable can be any kind of cord, twine or strand that is made of cotton, jute, or any other synthetic material. It comes in a variety of sizes and colors as well as spins. In this video we discovered that three-quarter" cotton string helped the rope has clotheslines.

* Service: You may need some thing for you to link to. Dowel sticks are a popular choice hoops, branches or bands. We

utilized dowel rods to tie all of these knots.

Crucial Macrame States

There are only two or three major ones that you can think of for Macrame needs you should be aware

of before you begin.

\* Work string the cable or a pair of strings that you use to make the knots you want.

• Filler cables: the cable, or the pair of cables that your knots are wrapped around.

* Senet: a knot or group of knots that may be utilized in duplicate.

Cord Measurement

Before you begin the macrame design it is crucial to determine the number of cords you'll require. This means knowing the size of your required cord as well as the total amount of items you need to buy.

Equipment: To measure, you'll require writing paper as well as a pencil, tape ruler, and calculator. Additionally, you'll need an understanding of units conversions that are described below:

* 1 inch equals 25.4millimeters equals 2.54 centimeters.

* 1 foot equals 12 inches.

* 1 yard = 3 feet = 36 inches.

* 1 yard = 0.9 meters.

Note the circumference of a rings is 3.14 * diameter, measured over the entire ring.

Measuring Width

The first thing to get is the final width of the largest part of your project. Once you've got this width, you need to write it down. Then, calculate the dimensions of the material by taking their length across the entire length. Then, identify the knot you want to use based on the understanding of this knot's pattern. You should know the width and spacing (if needed) of every knot. It is also important to determine whether you'd like to use more cords in order to expand an area or will require more cords to damps. By using the formula provided above, determine the circumference of the ring in your design. Decide on the technique of mounting to use. The cord may be affixed to rings, dowels or any other cord. Cords that are folded affect its length and the size measurement.

## Cord Preparation

While it isn't often mentioned but the process of preparing the cords and making them suitable for usage in macrame-related projects is considered to be one of the fundamental elements of the Macrame art. There are times when specialized processes like conditioning and stiffening of the cords are required prior to Macrame projects can begin. However, in general the preparation of cords in Macrame is focused on the cutting of ends and keeping them from unravelling in the course of the project. In the course of an undertaking, the constant handling of materials may result in a distortion of the ends. This can result in disastrous effects on the project. Before you begin your project, if do not properly prepare certain types of cords like ones created by the weaving of individual strings this cord will break completely, thereby ruining the project.

Thus, the preparation of cords is crucial and essential for your success with any Macrame project. The making of every single cord intended to be completed in the initial step of making a knot. This is the process where you cut your preferred length of cord out from your larger piece.

To condition your cord experts recommend applying beeswax across the length of the cord. In order to condition the cord just take a small amount of beeswax and let it warm up in your hands, then rub it all along the length of your cord. This will stop unwanted curly curls on your cord. It is important to note that beeswax can be used on both organic and synthetic substances. For synthetic materials, the only options are Satin or fine Nylon cords for beading require conditioning. After conditioning, you should inspect your cords for any flaws and eliminate any pieces that are not needed to ensure the perfect finish of your work. After conditioning, comes the actual procedure of preparing the cord. Cords can be made (i.e. the ends are protected from fraying) with the help of knots, a torch tape, glue, or knot.

To avoid unravelling of your cord with a torch first, test a tiny portion of the cord using the flame of the lighter of a small size. The material should melt, not to burn. If it does burn, this cord is not suitable for preparation of flames. To prepare the cord using a flame just hold the cord until the point of the fire for about 2 to 5 seconds. Ensure that the cord doesn't ignite but instead melts. This method is suitable for cords made of nylon, polyester, and olefin and is required for the making parachutist cords. Tieing knots at the ends of the cord can be an efficient way to avoid fraying. The knot overhand is the most popular knot, but knots such the figure-8 knot, which is ideal for flexible cords are an option when you are concerned that it will have to be re-tied at some point during the course of your work. The Stevedore knot is a good choice to stop fraying when working with slippery materials.

Glue is a different, priceless option which can be utilized to avoid fraying at ends of cords effectively. But, not all types of glue are suitable to prepare cords. Certain brands, such as Aleen's Stop Fray are suitable for cord preparation. Homemade glue can be utilized however only when it is dilute by water. To make your cord, apply the glue to both ends of your cord and allow it to dry. If you are planning to pass beads along the glued edge you can roll the cord's ends through your fingertips to narrow it after it has dried. Nail polish could be utilized in lieu of glue. Tape is also an effective method of preparing your cords. Wrap it around the top of the cord wherever you wish to stop the fraying of the material. Make sure that the top of the cord stays as slim by pressing them between the fingers. It is recommended to make use of masking tape or cellophane tape for the preparations. A specific category that includes Macrame cords, also known as parachute cables requires a specific type of preparation. Parachute cords consist of many core yarns, wrapped in a braided sleeve. To prepare a parachutist cord (also called a paracord) remove the yarns that make up the core from the sleeve and expose the yarns for about one-half inch. Then, cut the core yarns in such a way they are identical to the outer sleeve. then pull the sleeve forward until the yarns are completely invisible. For final preparation Apply heat onto the outer sleeve until it is melted, then use the handle of the lighter on the sleeve when it's still warm . This will help to smooth the surface and seal it up. The area that is melted will appear like it's darker and more plastic than the other parts in the fabric.

# Chapter 2: Tips For Macrame
## Beginning Macrame

Begin With Basic Knots

There are a myriad of knots, which can be difficult to master if you're new to playing. We recommend starting by learning a couple of basic knots and patterns to learn the ropes. One of the best knots to master is a basic square knot. The square knot forms the foundation of almost all macrame that is available and is an extremely easy beginner knot to learn. It is a knot that everybody is taught in our classes!

## Participate in A Workshop

It's fun to teach yourself If you're fortunate enough to have one in your area, we would suggest attending workshops. You will meet numerous like-minded individuals and take home your own piece of art and new acquaintances! We will be taking full US workshops tour in the summer. We will teach wall hanging mobiles, plant hangers as well as chandeliers, headpieces and much more! Visit the tour page to discover a city in your area.

Recycle Your Cords Left Over

As you learn, you be able to make a few attempts and retry. Finding the right length of the cord just right could be the biggest issue. It is not advisable to cut the cord because it could be difficult to add more to your project. We recommend that you always insist at minimum 10 percent more than what you think you'll need for safety reasons.

In the brand new Modern Macrame book, we have a step by procedure to figure out the amount of rope you will need to make your macrame.

It is important to keep in mind that you could have to deal with additional cords at the end the project! But don't fret! We would recommend saving all your cords that are left. It is possible to incorporate the cord into any future projects If you stay on the lookout, we will be going to launch a special free pattern in the coming weeks. It's a great method to recycle your scraps.

Learn on the internet

If you're unable to join us in person at a class or online course, then watching online tutorials is a second option. Sometimes it's simpler to follow someone who shows you the steps (haha) rather than studying the instructions on the page. There are plenty of YouTube tutorials on the web.

Have Fun!

Making Macrame your own by expressing your creative side is among the most enjoyable aspects of the process! Don't put too much pressure on yourself. Let your imagination let your imagination take the lead and you'll create an original and stunning piece!

Seven Basic Knots You Need to Know How To Master

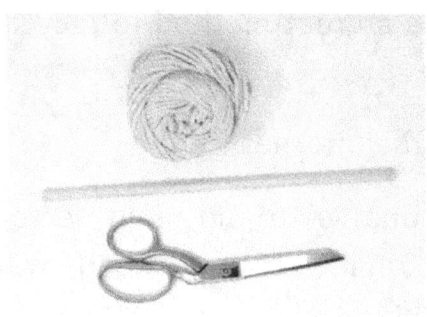

Reading to Knots Reading to Knot

When you're ready to begin studying macrame, make sure you have all the supplies and get familiar with commonly used macrame terms that you'll need to be aware of.

Materials and Supplies

Here's what you'll need in order to master and practice macrame knots:

* Macrame Cord It can be almost any kind of cord, twine or rope that is made from hemp, cotton Jute, synthetic material. It is available in a variety of sizes, colors and twists. In this example we will use 3/16" cotton cord that is sold as a clothesline rope.

• Support. You'll require some kind of tie to secure your knots. Dowel rods are a popular choice hoops, branches, or rings. We made use of a dowel rod to tie knots like these.

* Scissors

Important Macrame Terms

There are a few key macrame terms to be aware of before you begin.

* Working Cord A cord, or set of cables you use to tie the knots.

* Filler Cord A cord, or set of cables your knots will wrap around.

"Sennit": A knot, or set of knots made in a series of repetitions.

Lark's Head Knot

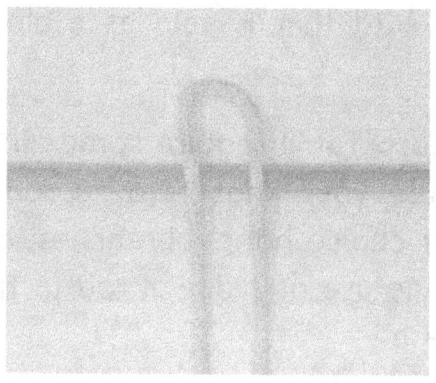

The knot you'll first need to master is the Lark's head Knot, sometimes referred to the Cow

Hitch Knot. This knot will keep macrame cords connected to an object like a dowel, branch or anchor cord.

Fold the cord in half, then place the loop on top of your dowel rod.

Loop the loop to the back, then pull the two cord ends through the loop until they are tight.

A reverse Lark's head Knot

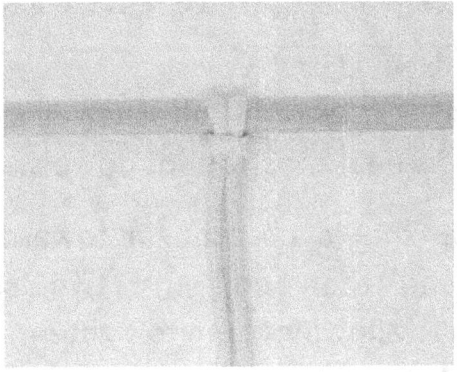

An Reverse Lark's Head Knot is made in reverse, which means that the bump is concealed in on the reverse of the knot.

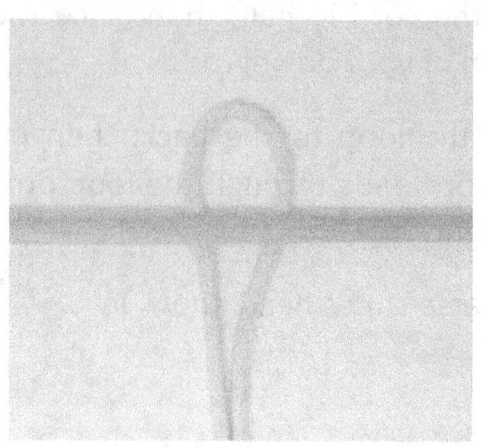

The cord is folded in half, then place the loop underneath the rod for dowels.

The loop should be brought towards the front, and then pull the two strings through it, allowing them to tighten.

## Square Knots and Half Knots

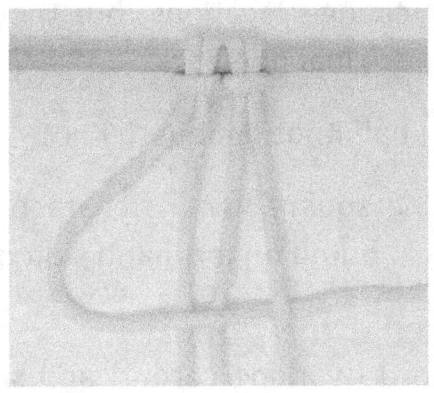

The square knot can be among the most commonly used macrame knots. It is possible to create it either right facing or left facing.

The half knot basically the half of the square knot. It may be facing right or left facing, based on which side you are on.

Square knots require at least four cords (2 working cords and two filler cords) however, they can be equipped with more. The first and final cords are called working cords. They'll be referred to as working cords 1 and 4. Middle cords will be filler and we'll name them 2 and 3. The cords will change locations, but they will keep their original numbers.

Left facing half Knot or Square Knot

A left-facing square knot is characterized by a vertical bump on left hand side of the knot.

The 1st cord (working cord 1) and shift it to the right , over those middle filler cords (filler cords 2 and 3) and then under the final cord (working cord 4).

Use working cord 4 to shift from left to, under the filler cords, and then over the working cord 1.

Pull both of the working cords to tighten, while keeping those filler cords in a straight line. This is a left-facing quarter square knot.

These working cords have changed places, and working cord 1 is on the right , and working cord 4 to the left. Work cord 1 is now taken and place it on the left, over two filler cords as well as under the working cord 4.

Work cord 4 is taken and shift it to the right , under the filler cords, and then over the working cord 1.

Pull both of the work cords to tighten. Make sure the filler cords are straight. This completes your left-facing square knot.

Right-facing half Knot as well as Square Knot

A right-facing half knot or square knot have vertical bumps to the left of the knot.

The last cord (working cord 4) and then move from left to right above two filled-in cords (cords 2 and 3) and underneath one of the cords (working cord 1,).

Use working cord 1 to move it to the right below the filler cords, and then over the working cord 4.

Pull both cords together to tighten and keep the knot straight. This is a right-facing quarter square knot.

These working cords have changed places, so that working cord 1 can be found on the right side and the working cord is to the left. Move working cord 4 to the right, under the filler cords and below working cord 1.

Use working cord 1 to shift from left to right moving it under the filler cords , and over the working cord 4.

Make sure you pull both cords in the same direction to tighten. This is a right-facing square knot.

Spiral Stitch

A Spiral stitch, also known as the Half Knot Sinnet or Half Knot Spiral is a set of half knots in order to make spiral stitches. It's a beautiful knot that can add a lot of visual interest to your project.

A spiral stitch requires at least four cords: 2 working cords and two filler cords. However, there are many more options. Visually count these cords from 4 to 1-4, moving from the left hand to left.

Your cords are 1 and 4. They are work cords, while cords 2 and 3 are your filler cords.

These instructions show how to create a left facing spiral stitch. However, you could also begin from the left side, and then use the right-facing half knots.

Use working cord 1 to shift it to the right under the filler cords, but underneath the working cord 4.

Transfer working cord 4 on the left moving through the filler cords, but over the working cord 1.

Pull both work cords to tighten those filler cords.

Continue to make half knots using the same method like above. As you continue to work the cords will begin to spiral.

Clove Hitch

A Clove Hitch or the Double Half Hitch can create lines within your work. They can be constructed in three ways: horizontally, diagonally and occasionally vertically.

Horizontal Clove Hitch

A Horizontal Clove Hitch is an array of knots that cross your macrame design. The initial cord acts as the filler, and the all the other cords are work cords.

Pick up the left end of your cord also known as the one that fills it, then then hold it horizontally between all the cords.

Next, take the cord (your first cord for work) and move it upwards, forwards and over the filler cord toward the left side to create the counter-clockwise loop.

Make use of the same cord, and then to the right of the knot that was tied make sure you pull it upwards, up and under the loop. You should now have two knots right next to each other. This is the vertical clove knot.

Repeat the clove knots using the following working cord to match the filler cord. Continue to tie knots until you get the appearance you desire.

Diagnol Clove Hitch

A Diagnol Clove Hook creates an array of diagonal knots that you can weave into your work.

Pick the cord to the left side, the filler cord, and then hold it in a diagonal fashion across each of the others.

Repeat steps 2 to four of horizontally arranged cloves, but moving diagonally instead of straight across. Repeat until you achieve the style you desire.

Overhand Knot

It is also known as the Overhand Knot is a basic knot that joins several cords together. It can be tied with several cords or one cord.

The cord should be folded into loop.

Connect the cords' ends through the loops to tighten.

Gathering Knot

An Gathering Knot, also called a Wrapping Knot is a knot that joins cords. They are often found on the bottom hanging macrame plants. Two cords are used for working in this knot. The remainder of the cords serve as filler cords.

Choose a separate piece of cord (this is your work cord) and create the loop in a

U-shape over the top of the set of filler cords. Make sure that the loop facing downwards.

Starting at the bottom of your cord that is pointed upwards, wrap them around filler cords as well as the loop. Be sure to leave a tiny bit of the loop untied.

Make sure you pass the end of your rope through the loop that is at the top of the wrapping.

Pull the end of the work cord--which is hanging from the top--upwards. This will place the loop in the wraps. Make sure the entire loop is encased within the wraps.

The knot you've been gathering is finished! If you'd like to, trim the ends of the cord to create a neat look.

## Chapter 3: Macrame Cord

If you're just beginning to learn about macrame, you'll usually be doing lots of study on the subject of macrame cord. It can be difficult to differentiate between the different kinds of macrame cords and which one that is suitable for you.

Macrame cord is a collection or collection of fibers/strands that are twisted or braided. It can then be tied or knotted to create a form of art known as macrame.

There are many instances where people refer to macrame rope as or as cords, macrame yarn or strings. This is due to the fact that macrame cord is used in conjunction with these terms.

Selecting Macrame Cord

It is difficult for novices to comprehend what each word really is. Therefore, it is best to go over the different kinds of macrame cords you must be aware of. This way, you will be capable of choosing the correct cord for future macrame-related projects.

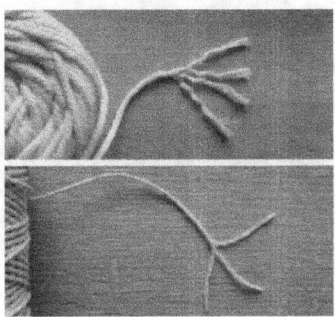

Three types of Macrame cords are:

* Braided

* 3ply * 3 Strand

* Single Strand

Most macrame projects fit into one of these categories.

Macrame Braided Cord

Braided cord, often referred to Macrame rope is your regular macrame cord is available at large-box retail stores. Most beginners start by purchasing braided cord as it is the most cost-effective and easiest method of starting macrame. It is typically the cord that can be found in a variety of craft stores as well as big box stores. A lot of people head to their local stores to buy any cord they can get in order to start immediately. After having completed a few macrame designs, they'll quickly realize that braided cord isn't the best type of cord to create macrame. This is because it is actually rope made either in its own form or as a mixture of cotton, nylon, polypropylene or other sturdy fibers. It's ideal for tying things together and providing an incredibly strong hold, however it is difficult to unravel and twirl with.

In the end, braided cord isn't an ideal way to start. It will get the job done and can leave you with a beautiful and well-finished project. In many instances you'll end up switching to 3ply, or even the more widely employed macrame cord, single cord.

There are many instances of cord and macrame rope and cord, but they're usually talking about the same thing. What I mean by distinguishing between them is that cord is generally braided, or 3-ply cord, and cord is a broader term used to describe fibers, strings and rope.

Macrame 3-Ply/ 3-Stands Cord

3-ply is also known as 3-stands cord. It is made up of 3 smaller strands joined together to create a huge knotted rope. It is common to hear macrame artists talk about using three-ply, or four-ply macrame cords and it is simply the number of strands that are twisted together to create one cord. Under the hood, you'll be able to see the difference between 3-Ply and 4-Ply.

As you progress into macrame cords that have longer than 3 strands it is called multi-ply. which means you have 4 six, five or six strands that are all spun together to create one single strand. You can clearly see in the picture above the four strands are joined to create one strand of rope.

Macrame One Strand of Cord

Single strand cotton cords are extremely the most suitable macrame cord available in the event that you want to take macrame seriously as a hobby on a regular basis or a full-time job. Single strand cords are generally more expensive, and should you not wish to spend money on expensive cord, look for lower-cost cotton cords on Amazon and begin with those. If it's easy on your hands, it'll be an excellent learning tool. It makes it simpler to cut cord, unravelling knots, knotting knots and even fringing the cord.

Now that you've a better awareness of the 3 different kinds of macrame cords Let's look at 4 crucial points that you need to look for when choosing which macrame cord is best for the macrame project you are working on.

Composition of Macrame Cord

Synthetic or Natural Fiber

Macrame cord is divided in two parts: Synthetic or Natural fibers.

Natural fibers are those that occur naturally by the natural environment. They are made by plants, animals or by geological processes. Jute, cotton, linen hemp, hemp, and wool are all examples of natural fibers.

Each of these fibers is easily broken down and reused.

The alternative can be synthetic fibers. Synthetic fibers are made from the synthesized polymers of smaller molecules. The chemicals used to create synthetic fibers originate from the raw materials like petroleum-based chemicals, or petroleum-based chemicals. Polyester, nylon, and spandex are a few examples of synthetic fibers.

Macrame Cord Texture

Macrame's texture, feel appearance, finish and texture

If you've ever been through a variety of macrame cords, then you'll notice that each spool of cord has a distinct feel, texture, and finish to it. Knowing the various types of texture is an essential part of knowing the macrame cords you have.

The more macrame-like pieces you create, the quicker you'll learn that textures play an important part in your macrame-related projects.

If you're planning to buy macrame cord , you should try various brands and suppliers to see which one you like the most. It will be apparent there are many different macrame cotton cords all created identical. The texture and feel of the cords can differ from one manufacturer to another.

Macrame Cord Size

Length and Diameter

The size of the cord is important when you are creating your macrame project of choice. The size of the cord is a crucial factor in the design of macrame projects.

To make it easier Macrame cords can be divided to three sizes namely small medium, large, and small.

1. The Small Macrame Cord - is classically your 1-2 mm diameter cord. It is common to see these strings used in the making of

jewelry that is threaded through buttons and beads and in small-detailed crafts.

2. Medium Macrame Cord is where the majority of macrame projects. It's usually between 3mm and 5mm. In general, you will frequently choose either 3mm or four millimeters. These sizes are often used for hanging planters and wall hangings, as well as curtains, lanterns, rugs and so on.

3. The Large Macrame Cord These will be the largest macrame pieces. It's a range of 6mm and over. In general, these sizes are used to cover large amounts of space. The knots are usually smaller, however, they're much larger.

What Cord Should You Use To Macrame?

The answer is simple dependent on.

Personally, I'd recommend using 3mm to 4mm of Single Strand cotton Cord. If you've attempted some small projects with cheaper cord and are now ready to invest in a higher-end cord to complete better projects, then single-strand cord could be for you. If you're a newbie and would like to start using the finest cord as soon as possible and you're not sure how, you are able to do so.

The reason I recommend using a single strand cord is to enhance your macrame experience. Making knots and unraveling the cords will not be as much of a hassle. The cutting and fringing process will be easier, and in the end your macrame designs will be visually stunning.

Macrame Beginners Occasional Knotters

It is likely that everybody has reached the exact point on their macrame journey therefore my suggestions might not be suitable for all. If you're brand novice to the art I suggest you use any rope you have lying around to learn. If not, you can purchase inexpensive cords from your local craft shop If you're keen to start right away or purchase some from Amazon. Use this cord to learn how to tie macrame knots patterns, patterns, and sequences. Start with smaller macrame projects like keys chains and macrame feather patterns in order to master the art of making knots.

Macrame Lovers & Enthusiasts

If you are looking to improve your macrame knotting technique and also to show off your work I would suggest the highest standard 3mm-4mm Strand Cord. Cord.

The softness and ease of knotting, as well as the simple fringing creates the perfect type of macrame cord you can make use of. I use it for the majority of my macrame-related projects.

# Chapter 4: Macrame Practice Project

A few reasons why I recommend a "practice" experiment:

It is used to delay the time you wait to Macrame rope.

This will let you become familiar with different macrame knots as well as their names and the best way to use them.

When you've completed your journey of learning, you'll be extremely happy and determined to do more or you'll realize that this isn't the right path for you.

This training course will allow you to be certain to commit your time and money for the next step towards the initial "genuine" macrame business.

Macrame Projects you can make

Decide on the project you wish to create. Look through pictures of macrame online. You can search Etsy, Pinterest, and Google. Explore to discover the options available.

What kinds of macrame projects can I create? Begin with a small.

*plant holder

*Jewelry, including pieces of jewelry that choke or arm bands

*wall hanging

*book mark

*Key chain

Greater ventures may include:

*table sprinter

*hammock (spare an important venture similar to this for a different time)

*lighting apparatus

*rug

*headboard

*Garland or hitting

1.Decide on the type of task. Plant holders and inside decorations are two of the most popular start-up initiatives.

2.Where will it be? This will allow you to determine the size you're planning to achieve.

3.Find the style that is appealing you. More natural or symmetric with crisp lines and well distinct styles?

Where can you find Macrame Patterns

Once you've decided on the kind of job and what style appeals to you, it's time to search for an illustration. I found my sample on Etsy for less than $5.

There is no need to buy an instance. There are tons of YouTube videos that guide you through creating a vast array of ventures are sure to be a hit. Three main reasons why I decided to buy an example:

I was looking through Etsy to think about what kind of project I had to undertake and realized that buying things was an option possibility. I started looking in the mirror at an endeavor which was exactly the one I had in mind.

*Patterns are a very feasible option ($5-$10).

*I was thrilled by the thought of not having to work one to the next video, stopping and beginning it continuously. The constant disconnect from my computer was a bit unsettling to me.

What Macrame Pattern can you use?

I've had people contact me with their specific questions about my instance. If you want to narrow your search and have been captivated by this example, it's classified as "Four Of Diamonds" from Reform Fibers. The examples are available on Etsy.

Materials Required to make Macrame

If you are able to design your project, you'll be able to determine how much rope you will need. I realized that I must make use of cotton string that is typical but you are able to let your own style and taste to dictate in choosing your color and the material. They offer rope (or rope) on Etsy. However the product wasn't available in the amount or worth I wanted. After much checking here, I found the connection I made.

To give you a hint the macrame I made called for 220 feet 1/4" (6 millimeters) 3 cotton rope.

Here's a list of the numerous things you'll require:

*Cotton macrame line (rope)

*Metal dowel or wood or similar tree limb , or flotsam and jetsam (for an progressively natural appearance) If you're working on dividers.

*Hanging ring to make an holder for plants

*Scissors

*Tape measure

*Tape (I used painters tape that was not difficult to get rid of, but covering tape would also work fine)

*If you do not want to use tape, you could "seal" your closures melting the finishes with a torch as an alternative.

Moving racks for clothing (or alternative method of hanging the venture, check underneath)

Alternatives to the best way to hang Your Macrame Project While You Are Working

*Under supplies , I recorded "moving the dresser rack." This is what I did and the way it was suggested but it's expensive and can be a bit costly in the event that you don't have one.

*You are able to work with your dowel, or the ring you hang from anywhere that's beneficial.

You can hang it from a door handle cabinet handles or wherever you locate to be sure of the quality of your item.

Another option is to use the pull cup snare, or an over-the-doorway wreath holder.

You can also add some of the craftsmanship by using your divider (briefly) and then balance your nail from your piece.

All Your Macrame Questions answered:

Can macrame be cleaned?

Yes, macrame is durable and will not break with any issue. It's possible that it was machine washed at 86 ° F in a small suitcase. Dry it.

Are you able to make use of yarn as a macrame?

Truly. You can utilize yarn. The only thing you need to remember is how big macrame piles can be the same depending on the yarn or material you select. The thinner the string yarn or string you select the smaller the bundles will be. If the yarn isn't enough, the clusters won't appear evident. The yarn could be the material that is ideal for an individual macrame project to make adornments for instance, and not larger projects such as tapestry.

Do you think you could macrame jute using macrame?

Truly. Jute and hemp were once thought to be well-known among macrame artists but their inaccessibility on the market allowed them to use macrame strings made from silk rayon, nylon and other synthetic filaments. For students the nylon or cotton strings are suggested due to the fact that they are easier to unravel due to confusion.

What should I consider when choosing which macrame rope to choose to complete my project?

There are many interesting aspects when choosing your materials. Cost and accessibility are always something to be considered. But, as you can imagine you might also need to take into consideration what is the best quality material you choose for your project. If you're planning the plant to go up such as, you'll have to select a stronger rope, such as those made of jute or calfskin cotton, nylon or lace.

Furthermore, you have be aware of the strength of your rope. For embellishments, you'll have to select a more lightweight and flexible rope such as weaving line, which is constructed of cotton , and is very soft and flexible. If you are planning to make an outdoor project, such as an open-air outdoor lounger or plant holder, you may need to select the polypropylene rope which is strong and durable.

What length of rope would be beneficial for me to make use of?

Based on your project, the best option is to pick the thickness of 4.0 millimeters or greater for larger ornaments like interior ornaments as well as plant holders. For smaller-scale macrame projects like arm bands or pieces of jewelry, you should pick a lines that are less than 2.0 millimeters across.

How much rope do I require to macrame?

The strings you utilize for hitting ought to be five times to multiple times the length of the entire length. These are the strings that you will use as the "center" ropes are used to create the form.

But if you are not actually hitched, the length might just be around twice the length of the finished length. Be sure to leave extra rope length to create a the periphery, or for other options to embellish at the ends. It's also better to have a large amount of rope than nothing. It is common to reduce long pieces towards the edge.

How can I ensure that my groups are uniform?

The best method to ensure your bunches are even is to ensure that you keep the tension on your ropes evenly and that every bunch aligns in a straight line on every side, on the same level that is slanting and vertically. Particularly if you are just beginning to learn, you must examine each group and make sure that it is in line to the process tie and and that edges are solid and the circles are also even. The best method to ensure that your project will be completed on time is to be sure of your project. For larger projects, you'll have to hang them on a rack for clothes or from a secure snare. Most likely, you

How do keep my group looking uniform?

The best way to ensure that your groups are even is to make sure that you keep the tension on your ropes equal and that each group aligns in a straight line on all sides, in a straight plane, horizontally, and corners to corners. Particularly when you're just beginning to learn, you must inspect each and every bunch to ensure that it matches an appropriate procedure tie. Also, ensure and that the edges are solid and that the circles are evenly. The best way to ensure that your undertaking will be even is to ensure the project. For larger projects, you'll require hanging them on a rack for clothes or from a secure snare. In the ideal scenario, you can balance your project with two main points with the intention that the project doesn't move around. For smaller tasks like gems , you'll need to build a macrameboard.

What is a macrameboard?

Macrame boards are the place you can ensure the project you are planning to tie. It is made of a variety of materials, but in the end you must create an even surface that allows you to put pins on. You could use the plug board or even a piece of polyurethane, or two pieces of cardboard that are joined. The board should measure 12 inches in size and sturdy enough to put an a corsage or T pin inside without it extending to on the other side.

What is the reason why macrame is making the rebound?

Macrame was a well-known style with a focus on the 1970's when it was a part of the radical culture, however it has come back into fashion as part of the current traditional or Boho (Bohemian) pattern patterns of home styling design.

What was the first place that macrame began?

Macrame is believed to be derived of macrame, which is the Arabic phrase "migramah" which translates to "periphery" and is a reference to the 13th century custom used by Arabic weaver to construct more boundaries on ponies and camels to prevent the tidal waves from the animals.

It may also come out of its Turkish phrase "makrama" meaning the word "napkin" or "towel. Macrame was used to make certain of the edges of lingering texture. The most frequent recorded instances of macrame were found in brightening carvings of Babylonians as well as the Assyrians.

Macrame was popular during the Victorian period, when houses were embellished by this particular style of decoration in items like decorative quilts, decorative liners and draperies. In the 17th century, the reigning queen Mary even gave macrame instructions to her female guests in pausing. Macrame was also a highly popular side-interest of British as well as American mariners of the nineteenth century who produced small-scale specialties were often sold or trade ports for.

# Chapter 5: Tools And Materials Utilized In Macrame Macrame Materials

Macrame stylists employ various types of materials. Materials are classified into two main categories The natural and synthetic materials.

* Natural Materials

The properties of natural materials differ from those of synthetic materials and understanding these differences will assist you in making the best use of these materials. Natural cords that are available in the present include Jute, Hemp, Leather Silk, Cotton, Silk and Flax. Also, you can find yarns created of natural fibers. The natural material fibers can be produced from animals and plants.

* Synthetic Materials

As with natural substances, synthetic materials are often used in macrame designs.

The synthetic fibers are produced by chemical processes. The main ones are nylon beads, satin cord, olefin along with parachute cord.

General Supply

1. Macrame Project Board

A task board is created by gluing sheets foam or cork. So long as it's sufficiently thick to keep those pins sticking to of the back of the board, it can be suitable for a macrame task.

2. Tweezers

Tweezers can also be used to create ornamental work. A set of tweezers could be utilized to help excellent knot threads that are woven into beadwork.

3. Scissors

16

A great set of sharp scissors is able to cut threads in Macrame tasks specifically. There are a variety of sizes and grips to make it easier. You can consider buying one that comes with a sheath protector to ensure the blades are secured.

4. T-Pins

T-Pins serve to attach the thread or macrame yarn to the board that is being installed.

The ones made of steel are stronger and last to longer use.

5. Pattern

There are a myriad of things you can accomplish using macramefrom bags to baby mobiles. Macrame patterns give detailed directions for knots to use as well as measurement guides and the final assembly instructions.

Macrame is an old Arabian weaver's art that was used to weave decorative fringes onto objects like veils wraps, and bath towels. Today the belts, wall hangers as well as plant wall mounts along with fashion accessories are created using this knotting technique.

## 6. Needles

Needles can also be used along with macrame. Needles are used for assembling the finished work and also to beadwork.

Cords and Beads

Cording types

C-Lon - My patterns utilize the cord C-Lon Bead Cord. It's a three-ply nylon cord, which is similar with Conso or Mastex Nylon #18. It offers an extensive range of colors, and has a less expensive cost per spool. This is the standard size for jewelry made of micro macrame. It's offered in smaller dimensions.

Tuff is also a three-ply nylon cord, it's offered in 16 different colors, and different sizes. It is not pliable or stain and also resists fraying. Size 5 is similar in size to the C-Lon beading cord.

17

D&E (formerly Mastex no. 18) Cord of nylon originally created for the upholstery industry. It is flexible and soft. Available in around 17 colors.

Beads types

Metal - These are not precious metals that provide an alternative that is less costly than gold and silver.

Crystal - It's the result of the numerous cuts on the surface of glass that give crystal the appearance of fancy.

Glass - This is where you'll discover lamp and flame work beads.

Affordable and versatile Glass beads are the ideal choice for new beaders.

Semiprecious (or gemstone) They are popular because they provide a wide range of choices. The options are numerous but here are only a handful options: amber, agate garnet, jade and onyx.

clay – These bead could be made of clay, which is then fired in a kiln before being it is then glazed. Or, they can be made from porcelain, and usually includes a potter's tool, an oven, and hand-painting. Polymer clay can also be used which is not actually a clay however it is a plastic. This is an oven baked clay that is used at home to create individual beads. It is extremely adaptable.

Additional - Other-There are shell-based beads like mother-of-pearl, tigershell, conch shells and abalone. There are also wooden beads that are made from the roots, bark or branches of a variety of kinds of trees. Some of the wooden beads are designed and are popular for many generations.

18

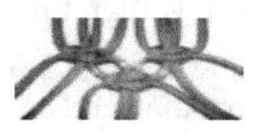

# Chapter 6: Is It Possible To Create An Business Today With Macrame?

MAcrame could also be an opportunity for you to start your own small-scale business. Once you have mastered your Macrame abilities, you are able to easily sell your products and earn a good amount for your items, particularly in the event that you are able to make products like bracelets that customers purchase a lot of. You can also train others and create your own business that creates custom Macrame accessories for fashion. The possibilities that Macrame offers are infinite.

The most efficient method to Macrame

If you're looking to know how to make Macrame there are numerous places to go. Making intricate knots creates stunning examples that could be transformed into stunning jewellery, flower boxes and wall decors. the things that Macrame is primarily focused on as a form of art. The very first and least confusing step in trying to figure out how to make Macrame if you're interested in this subject, is to comprehend the basic knots and two diagrams.

The internet is a great source to begin searching for ways to learn how to macrame. Visual guides are of immense aid and can help you figure out how to Macrame easy. For a lot of people, it's significantly easier to follow diagrams than written instructions which can be extremely difficult to comprehend. In addition, once you've become familiar with visual aids and diagrams, it's time to learn the steps to begin the process of Macrame.

Drawing a diagram and not paying attention to how comprehensive and well-detailed it is, doesn't provide much assistance to you have the ability to properly Macrame. It is essential to have the right string in order in order to effectively Macrame. As with all art that is purchased trying to understand the best way to Macrame is also a matter of practicing. Find some clear, well-constructed representations of the basic diagrams to start. You'll find the simpler ones as being less complex than the more complicated contemporary diagrams. There is the possibility to move into them after plenty of effort and time.

Apart from the basic knot patterns You also be able to choose to focus and practice some time before you are able to recall the exercises and create the symmetrical knots. It's not a good idea to learn this if you're in a hurry and require to go step by step to learn how to Macrame. After you've completed the knots that are the main ones will be in place. keep arranging them in order to make important works such as bracelets. Alongside knots, you also need to keep an eye on how to choose the most appropriate colorings for the knots.

Wristbands can be a great aid for those who are just beginning as they provide knots that are the easiest to tie require no degree of complexity. Once you are more confident in your abilities, you will be able to perform extremely good examples. The greatest benefit of mind-boggling and extremely confounding strategies is the fact that they are able to be developed to create complex things that appear extraordinary.

The time it is needed to determine the best way to Macrame will depend on a variety of aspects like how quickly you are able to learn the method. If you've been sewing or knitting for some time The complexity should to be less as there are some similarities with the method.

Macrame Today

The macrame of the present is a new shade palette. If someone is intentionally duplicated the 70's for the purpose of coordinating their retro shag covers, it's generally made of different shades typically pastels, whites and earth-tones. But that isn't a good idea Macrame is a design that can be created in a variety of styles. It's usually gorgeous knotwork.

We are a retailer that offers different kinds of ropes for creating and other ropes, we at Paracord Planet are a little surprised when customers browse our website for the term "macrame cord." In the past, hemp and cotton rope was considered to be healthy. But since those were the ropes of the day. whatever you want.

In its most recent rebound, synthetic filaments are often used including paracord. Other macrame strings include cotton rope that is engineered to form a chain manila/hemp ropes, jute and even the calfskin. Any type of cable can be considered macrame rope. I'm sure at some moment, the leading edge will look at macrame of the present and view it as outdated and ask how we can imagine that something this unattractive could ever be beautiful just like we used to treat our grandparents.

It's easy to get started in macrame. It's a broad category of art, and anyone is able to find a activity that suits their tastes. For starters this, we have two macrame-related instructional exercises are currently available for download.

Where can I locate Macrame Patterns?

When you've determined what kind of job and style appeals to you then you're ready to search for an idea. I found my routine on Esty for less than 5.

You don't have to buy an idea. There are a Gazillion YouTube images that can aid you in the creation of many projects that you will surely love. The three main reasons why I chose to purchase a plan could be that I had been looking through Esty to find ideas on what I wanted to create and came to the point where buying patterns could be a viable option. I was enthralled by the results that are exactly what I had been thinking about. The patterns are a very affordable option ($5-$10).

I liked the concept of not having to be working side-by-side on an image, then switching it off and on frequently. Unplugging my personal computer was more relaxing for me.

You can keep your hands busy with macrame

This is because home-based activities allow people to remain active and involved throughout the outbreak. A large portion of Americans spend an enormous amount of time in their homes because it has irritated them. We're looking for ways to revive old hobbies or begin new ones. Everyone, whether old or young, must do something else with their appearances. We are all in search of something exceptional. We are drawn to something that is unique and isn't found anywhere else.

In actuality there's seen a surge in demand for a wide range of crafts and activities (as in the realm of musical toys and instruments) as, in the words of an digital marketing firm that studies these patterns, a greater amount of people are experiencing isolation, or self-isolation "art or craft shops" are thought to be more significant in the present, as they can encourage pleasure in self-isolation and isolation cycles. Hand-crafted (and hand-crafted) products are available either online or at a store or, with the help in DIY kit kits you are able to make the art of making them by yourself. Customers love it when you are able to show off the work you've put into it and be happy.

While people may be emotionally distant and unattached, they tend to look back at the positive effects of depression as well as the decrease in anxiety.

Consider the macrame knotted artwork and you're likely to dream of delicate, soft wall hangers and plant holders and plant holders. You can still find plants and wall hangings but in a modern way in the present. The art is now featured every kind of furniture and furniture for your home such as rotating chairs, desks tables, and even table runners. It is also possible to see them in the reception of your grandchild or child--draped on the backs of benches, or as backdrops for the photo booth or in the ceremony's dress code.

Macrame today is reimagined as more than the white or beige. Take into consideration the influence of ombre (fading from one shade of paint to the next) and vibrant, energetic hues. There are many different products nowadays than the standard brown jute. Twine hemp, cotton cord and even the material used in the production of t-shirts is packaging.

To make them unique It is also fun making macrame as well as coming up with various concepts and designs. The old art form is being resonant with the most recent version of. A lot of people who have fond memories -- or wish to take up the hobby for the first time, will appreciate Macrame as a fantastic activity and art form for safety and brain-boosting.

Earn Money by selling Macrame

A new twist has been added to the art form that was once lining homes with owls and plant hangers. These are calming and are always artistic.

Head of the Lark the cube, half-hitch horizontal double and so on. They all go backwards. It was a long time before these ties were thoroughly studied, but the macrame is still all around.

Home decor is always huge and the people have come to appreciate the style. Many have realized that they need to take a break from their televisions, as well as from some exhausting activities.

Since the 1970s the knotty clothing trend which was everywhere has been gaining momentum. People who love it purchase rope in large quantities as well as research trends and buy racks of clothes to hang the wall hangings once they're used. For those who aren't creative were renting the macrame backdrops to decorate the reception or just looking for boho furniture to purchase.

Macrame is currently making use of cotton rope mainly in chic or white shades rather than rough jute. It also has some sort of bohemian-glam style.

People are curious to know what's developed into Macrame and believe it's getting more modern. When you make use of Macrame it's simple to create those Christmas presents.

Medical student from the University of Minnesota says he was first interested in macrame as a method of delaying from school and has been using this "furiously." "It's extremely creative and meditative" I asked him. "It seemed pretty nice and appeared like quite an amount of study is necessary, but it's really straightforward."

The tradition originates from the ancient knot-work techniques from Chinese and other crafts made in the Arabian Peninsula by weavers of the 13th century. It was first introduced by sailors who made and sold macrame-related equipment. After a considerable amount of time, it gained popularity in the royal court of queen Mary, Katz wrote in her novel.

This was rediscovered throughout the US in the 1960s along with batik, tie-dyeing and decoupage, and became so well-liked that it was taught in schools. The popularity of this was evident during summer camps and was the subject of a variety of pamphlets and pattern books that helped decorate homes with macrame owls, knotted Jute decoration , and hangers for plants.

In 1973, as rope art was a hit with people across the world, a rope specialist thanked

The NY Times for its therapeutic advantages, noting that "It is evident the rope study isn't only being used by older people and children, but young adults as well."

In the fluorescent and flowering 1980s, macrame was out of fashion but made a fleeting return in the 1990s. Hemp bracelets and necklaces were suddenly fashionable, but then they weren't.

The new version is connected to the existing love for everything 1970s such as crafts and fun patterns within the field of interior decoration. It is also believed to be connected to the long-established fascination with home plants.

Two years ago 2 years ago, special paraprofessional education in Minneapolis required a macrame hanger to keep its expanding collection of plants however, she couldn't find one that was available for purchase. She decided to research ways to make one online and found some tutorials in German and they were able to figure them. She quickly got addicted.

In the present, as an extra project, she runs Macrame Company together with her partner and a roommate from her former college who's daytime job is selling merchandise. We make huge-scale tapestries for weddings and celebrations to rental or for sale. We also work with photographers throughout the region, and offer hanging plants that are ready-made for shops. The work is displayed in various local venues.

How do you Earn by selling your work on Etsy?

Macrame Knots You can make

It is important to ask whether learning about the various macrame knots actually have to do with hobbies. It's true, if you believe that making a variety of macrame knots is not a hobby. Let's express our appreciation for this particular and stunning pastime, and check out the macrame knots can we make.

Simple Methods to Tie Macrame Knots?

Review the steps below to discover how easy it reality, is to make knots. Look up Macrame plant wall mounting guidelines to learn more.

Square Macrame Knot

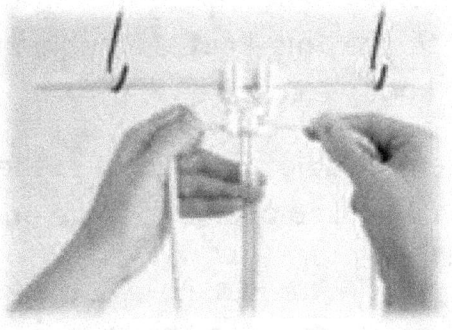

Get the exact orange cable, and then go below the red cable to the left.

Keep the cables in the same pattern starting from the right delegated cable green, orange, and red. Choose the most powerful Orange cable, and then cross it with green cable. For the knot you'll need three cables, red, orange and green as well as security pins, as well as cardboard.

Make sure you have all three cables by hand, and tie a knot over the top to join the cables. Make use of a security pin connect them back to the cardboard.

Make sure you connect both red and orange cables to complete the knot. Make sure to make this knot as similar to the original knot we created.

Take the red cable and place it to the cable in green. It will go over an orange one. This creates loop.

In the exact same manner, repeat the actions to make square knots the length you wish the string to last.

## Plaited Chain Stitch

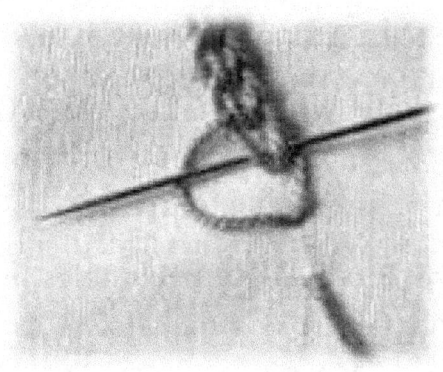

Keep the cables' pattern that are delegated right--pink and grey. Take the grey cable and discuss it over the purple and white cables. Then, take the purple cable, and talk about white and pink cables. Create a loop around each cable, and then make sure to pull them through.

To create this knot macrame it is necessary to have four cables in purple, grey white and pink and a security pin. You'll also need cardboard.

By knotting the cables it is possible to connect the cables. Pull the grey cable to the ground now, and then begin exactly the same steps using the pink cable.

Create a loop with two cables and then pull it through. Pass all four of them, and connect the grey cable to the left.

Make sure you have all four cables in your hands and tie an edging on top to keep them secure. Make use of a security pin fix them to the cardboard. By using this method, you'll move your way through the cables, and create macrame knots pendants or macrame bracelets.

The head of the Vertical Lark

Another element of the style that Macrame plants have on their wall mounted is the pot you choose to put the plant placed in. There are many types of options available and you can play with the colour of the pot and how it matches the hue or look of the plant and also the cable or rope is used to hang it using.

Different ways to use macrame Plant Hangers

It is possible to select a selection of plants that thrive outdoors and then construct an assortment of wall-mounted plants. The plant wall mounts and place them outside, such as on a terrace or patio. There are different designs and patterns you can weave the wall mounts with which you are able to customize the appearance of the wall mount by using different designs. Some patterns are more elaborate than others, for example some are more elegant, while others are simpler and more plain. They also have a the more basic or practical design. Choose the one which is most appropriate for the space that the wall mount will be placed within and then begin knitting away!

Another fantastic method of using Macrame wall mounts for plants is in rooms where you can benefit greatly from the tranquility and beauty they bring. Bedrooms can often be improved with the inclusion of a plant and it's really lovely to have a lovely plant in your bedroom , especially if you are spending a significant amount of time there.

How to Make Macrame Plant Hangers

The plant can be hung on the wall mount using a technique which highlights the netting and the plant by selecting a top rope or string to hang the plant and the pot into. It is also possible to experiment with joining knots of various types in the rope where the plant as well as the wall mount are placed to change the appearance and appearance of your wall mounted as a whole. A lot of people choose to make their wall mounts by knitting instead of using twine or rope and then connecting knots. It is a pleasurable but more challenging version of the task, and it's an excellent option in the event that you're a competent knitter. It's a lot longer to knit the wall-mounted instead of using twine or rope and so make sure you have the time and motivation to see the project through before you begin.

They're also excellent places to put up one or several plant wall mounts since they could end up becoming an excellent feature in the space and can enhance the view outside the conservatory, that is evident due to the numerous glass and windows that they have. In such a setting it is recommended to create a wall mount with gentle or light colors to ensure that it doesn't distract the surrounding from the observatory or in the interior of the area.

On the underside, using White cable you can bypass any dark blue cables then beneath it, then take it over it, and finally with the loop. Be sure to follow the cables in the same pattern as being delegated right-dark-white-blue and right-dark. The majority of the work is done through using the white cable. Place the white cable on top of the blue dark cable. Then fold it over and then run it through the loop.

To make this knot you'll need two cables of white and dark blue as well as a security pin and a cardboard.

Put both cables in one hand, then tie knots on the top to keep them secure. Make use of a security pin fix them to the cardboard.

This pattern has to be like: over, under through, under and through. All you need to do is replicate the same actions across the cables.

Plant Hanger

Price: $2.00-$2.95

People are beginning to appreciate the importance and benefits of having plants in the office or at home anywhere is possible. Macrame plant wall mounts could easily be created by DIY. If you choose to build the wall mount for a Macrame plant your self it is possible to make them very cheaply, and also.

# Chapter 7: The Tools Required To Run Macrame

Macrame Project Board

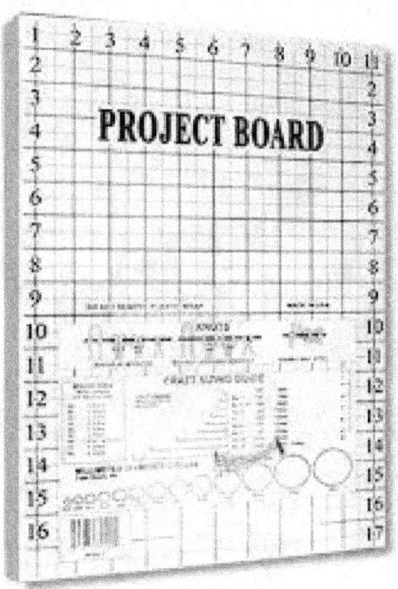

The project-mounting board can be the essential device to run macrame. This is your work place where you put your work. In art stores you will find boards that have grid-inch markings as well as appropriate directions printed on the sides. A project board can be made by gluing them together or using Cork Foam sheets. The board can be used for macrame projects insofar as it's sufficiently thick to keep that nails stick out in the back.

T-Nails

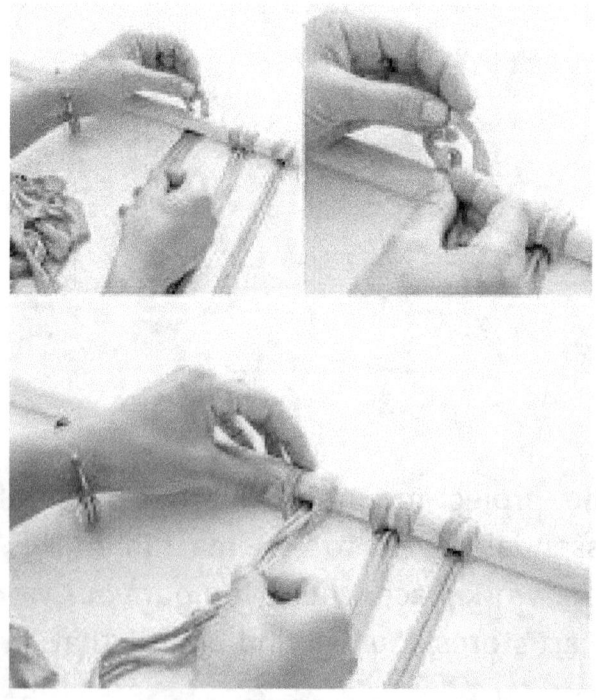

T-Nails can be used to anchor the rope or macrame yarn to the board for mounting. T-nails are available in different sizes. Smaller nails are ideal for smaller, more delicate designs. Nails are likely to break after a long period of usage. Steel nails are stronger and will last longer.

The cross-nail technique shown here is a great way to use nails to secure delicate ropes and not damage the ropes.

Pattern

Many things can be made using macrame, from bags to clothes. Most of the time, you'll require a template for macrame. Macrame patterns give step-by step guidance regarding the knots that should be used, instructions for calculating, as well as instructions for the final assembly. You can purchase patterns, you can also search for them on the internet.

Tweezers

Another tool that is used for decorative purpose is Tweezers. You can make use of the tweezers to aid in knotting good threads between beads.

Fine tip long noses Tweezers are great when you're working with fine ropes or beads.

Scissors

A sharp pair of scissors can be used to cut threads in a proper manner when using the macrame layout. There are various sizes and comfortable grips.

Needles

Needles are employed to ensure the alignment of the finished product as well as perforation. Based on the type of project it is recommended to utilize tapestry or blunt-end needles and pointed or Chenille needles. Specific measurements are made to accommodate yarn types such as nylon or silk, and for various beads that have been formed.

Measurement Tape

In order to complete a number of macrame projects measuring tape that is flexible is needed.

Tape and Cellophane

Cellophane tape and rolls are also useful and should be stored together with the other macrame materials.

As you can see below as shown below, you must apply tape to the tips of the ropes in order to prevent the ropes from twisting.

Beeswax

Natural materials might require a beeswax-based coating which helps maintain and soften the fibers.

String

To make jewelry, you'll need 1 mm to 2 mm string items.

Decoration

Pendants, beads, or clasps for micro-macrame may be necessary.

You might also be interested in macrame beads as well as animals eyes, circles and various other items.

Fabric Glue

It's simple to make use of fabric glue for designing and painting, therefore be sure you have a supply of glue.

Make sure that the adhesive is clear.

A BBQ Lighter

Do you prefer synthetic materials like nylon parachutist rope?

If you plan to light up the ropes, then you might need a barbecue lighter.

What is the difference between a Rope, a String Rope, a String, and a Cord

Macrame string is a silky single twist string similar to those that Niroma Studio has become famous for.

String expands faster than thread since it is able to unwind quickly, so the width of the whole will vary between 1 and 1.5 millimeters when it is damaged along the conduit after it splits. Some retailers may call it something different it is important to keep this in mind.

"What's the ideal macrame string for novices?" I am always asked this question about this, and I always pick the 5mm natural cotton string. It's the perfect size to hang on an attractive medium-sized wall and is more suitable than the 3mm, and it also has a compact medium twist as well as the ability to be delicately unknotted and then reknitted few times before it loses its elasticity, provided you're cautious. Being gentle on your hands is always a good way to keep yourself active!

Macrame ropes are typically three-strand rope in which it is wrapped with fibers around one other (sometimes called three-ply). It can also be found in four strands, however the most common rope is three strands. Macrame rope is typically more durable than macrame string and gives you lovely wavy fringes when you pull it off and is perfect for adding character to your work.

Because it is heavier because of its weight, I would prefer to use it in the areas of objects that require an enormous amount of weight. The macrame rope will stretch when cut, and based on the location you are in or how humid you're in and other factors. Additionally, it can expand up to 1cm.

Macrame cord is usually a six-strand (or greater) braided thread or, as I'm assuming, was the most popular choice from the 1970s until the in the early 1980s, when cotton string wasn't the 'it most appropriate' choice. The tightly-woven macrame rope made of cotton is often known as "sash rope." Sash rope can be a bit stiff to work with and difficult to take off, yet it is extremely sturdy, which means it's great for heavy-duty parts as well as if you're looking to add a lot of strength to the job you're doing. Macrame rope is not the best for hands, but if you're looking for a specific style or flexibility, you'll have to endure the minor discomfort.

Polypropylene (or polyolefin) macrame rope, which is great for outdoor use because it doesn't change shape as quickly as cotton. But, the edges could appear "frizzy," so that's the most important thing to consider.

Macrame Supplies

To construct your craft projects, macrame tools and other crafting equipment are required. Here is a list the essential items you require prior to starting any task.

You can purchase most of these items in art supply stores. However you may already have some at your home.

It is also recommended to have a table or alternative surface to work on.

A box or container where you can keep all the tools and equipment can also be useful. The cords employed in macrame are usually extremely long and you shouldn't allow your pets or children to get caught in them.

## Chapter 8: Macrame Knot Instructions

Macrame is an incredibly versatile craft that is versatile. It is used to create different kinds of jewelry, like bracelets, collars, and chocolates. It's also used to make things that are popular every day like hammocks, plant hangers and curtains.

Let's talk about how to create the macrame knots.

1. How to tie an half knot.

One-half knots are among the most basic macrame knots. A few of the most sophisticated Macrame knots, patterns and designs are based on this. Three components are needed to make the half knot. A core cord, stationary and knotting two cords externally.

The knotted string is placed on top of the middle one, and the knotting string used to form a half knot. Take the second string, and then follow both the middle string and it's predecessor string. Make sure to close the knot now. You've successfully completed a half macrame knot.

It's an abstract explanation of the connection of a half knot but how does it work? If you perform it correctly, the result is quick.

Step 1. Find the appropriate knotting cord that is in between your hands. It will create an right-hand loop.

Step 2. Use your left hand to tie the cord around the right string.

Step 3. Once you have knotted the hand left side, once your string is placed, you can twist it to the underside of one of the ropes for knotting the other hand. When you are in the right loop with your right hand and thumb index, connect your thumb and index fingers and attach them and place them on leave knotted rope.

Step 4. Make sure you pull the knot tight. If the middle string is sturdy, then you should be able to effortlessly draw the knot. If the middle string is not secure then you have to tie the knot. Each knot will take only minutes to tie.

2. How do I make a Square Knot.

Once you've learned to tie half knots but you need to be able to tie an asymmetrical knot. Because a square knot is linked to only two knots. We'll tie the half knot first, just like before. However, in the second part of the knot we'll begin with an additional knotting cable instead of using the knotting one.

Use the second knotting string, and cross it over the middle and then under the knotting string. Then take the first string and then go underneath the middle string, and then the other string. Pull hard. You've just tied the square knot.

3. Hand knot

Hand knots are an easy macrame knot. You can use a single string create an arm knot. Begin with a loop to complete your list. Put the string's end in between the loop and then string. Then, push it close.

4. Instructions for flat macrame templates.

The Macrame is a string of square knots that are consecutively connected the flat pattern.

5. Instructions for making a macrame spiral style.

Half knots are connected to macrame patterns. It is recommended that you tie your spiral with the total of at least four half knots.

6. Instructions to make the Josephine knot.

The Josephine knot is a complicated macrame knot that is advanced and complex.

Step 1. Start with cord A and convert the loop cord B.

Step 2. Begin by taking cord B. Over and above the first one Take cord A.

Step 3. Continue to transfer cord B to the second end of cord A.

Step 4. Bring cord B and cord A together.

Step 5. Begin pushing cord B to the level of cord B. Pass it over it.

Step 6. Next, take cord B off the outside of cord.

Step 7. Take all 4 cords together to tie the Josephine knot evenly.

# Chapter 9: How Do I Start The Process Of Starting A Macrame Project

The study of knots

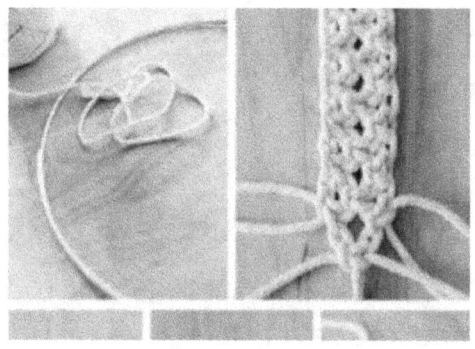

When you are ready to begin learning to Macrame make sure you have your tools and get familiar with some basic Macrame specifications that you'll be required to understand.

Materials and supplies

Here's the information you're going to learn and learn how to tie the Macrame knots you'll need to know:

Macrame cable is any cord, twine or strand of cotton, jute, or any other synthetic material. It is available in different sizes and colors as well as spins. In this article we have discovered that three-quarter" cotton string is the best option, as the rope with clotheslines.

* Service: You may need an item that you can link to. The most popular options are dowel sticks branches, hoops or bands. We utilized dowel rods for all of these knots.

Crucial Macrame States

Macrame rules you need be aware of prior to begin.

* The working string the rope or cable that you use to tie the knots you actually tie.

• Filler cables: it could be the cable or a pair of wires that your knots are wrapped around.

* Senet: a knot or group of knots that may be used in a duplicate.

Cord Measurement

Before you start the macrame design it is crucial to know the amount of cord you'll require. This means being aware of the size your required cord as well as the total quantity of items you need to buy.

Equipment: To measure, you'll need an article of writing paper and pencil, tape ruler and a calculator. Also, you will require basic understanding of units conversions as described below:

* 1 inch equals 25.4millimeters equivalent to 2.54 centimeters

* 1 foot equals 12 inches

* 1 yard = 3 feet = 36 inches

* 1 yard = 0.9 meters

Note The circumference of the band is 3.14 * diameter as measured across the rings

Measuring Width

The first step is to determine the final length of the broadest portion of your work. When you've got the width you want, write it down.

Then, figure out the size of the material by taking measurements of the width of the material across the entire length.

The next step is to identify the knot you would like to use, based on your information about this knot's pattern. It is important to know the length and spacing (if necessary) of every knot. It is also important to determine whether you'd like to increase the number of cords you have to increase the size of an area or the area, or if you will require more cords for damps.

Utilizing the formula above, you can calculate and calculate the diameter of the ring that you have chosen for your design.

Choose the method of mounting that will be used. The cord may be affixed to rings, dowels or any other cord. Cords that are folded affect their length as well as the width measurement.

## Cord Preparation

While it isn't often mentioned The preparation of cords and making them suitable for usage in macrame-related projects is considered to be one of the most important aspects of the Macrame art. There are times when specialized processes like conditioning and stiffening of the cords are required prior to when Macrame projects can begin. However, in general the preparation of cords in Macrame is focused on the cutting of ends and stopping them from breaking in the course of the project. In the course of any project, continual handling of materials could cause the ends to become distorted that could have negative consequences for the project. Before you begin your project, make sure you don't properly prepare specific kinds of cords like those made through weaving individual strings the cord could break, thereby ruining your project in the process.

So, preparation of the cord is crucial and essential for your success with any Macrame project. The making of every single cord intended to be accomplished prior to making a knot. This is when you cut your preferred length of cord out from your larger piece.

To help condition your cord experts recommend applying beeswax along the cord. For conditioning your cord just take a small amount of beeswax and let it warm up in your hands, then rub it all along the length of your cord. This will prevent unneeded tight curly curls that your cord may have. Be aware that beeswax can be applied to the natural as well as synthetic material. For synthetic materials it is the only Satin or fine Nylon beads require conditioning. After conditioning, you should inspect your cords for any flaws and dispose of any useless pieces to ensure the perfect execution of your work. After conditioning, comes the actual procedure of preparing the cords. Cords can be made (i.e. the ends are protected from fraying) by using knots, a torch tape, glue and a knot.

To stop unraveling the cord by using a flame first, test a tiny part of the material using the light from the lighter of a small size. The material must melt, not ignite. If it does burn, this cord is not suitable for preparation of flames. For preparation using a fire you simply need to hold the cord at the point of the fire for between 2 and five seconds. Ensure that the cord doesn't burn however it melts. This method is suitable for cords made of nylon, polyester, and olefin as well as required for the making of cords for parachute.

Tieing knots at the ends of the rope is an efficient way to avoid fraying. The knot overhand is the most popular knot, but knots such the figure 8 knot that are best suited for flexible cords are an option in the event that you believe it will have to be removed in the course of your project. The Stevedore knot is a good choice to avoid fraying with slippery materials.

Glue is a different, priceless option that can be utilized to avoid fraying at ends of cords effectively. But, not all types of glue are suitable to prepare cords. Certain brands, like Aleen's Stop Fray are suitable for cord preparation. Homemade glue can also be employed but only dilute by water. To make your cord ready you just need to rub the glue onto edges of cord and allow it to dry. If you plan to put beads across the glue end make sure to roll the cord's ends with your hands to narrow it when it is dry. Nail polish could be used in lieu to glue.

Adding Cords

Finishing Techniques

Finishing techniques are the process by which cords' ends when knots are made can be managed to make an orderly and neat project. Finishing is commonly described as knotting off. There are a variety of finishing knots widely available and offer incredibly efficient methods to finish procedures. The most reliable knots for finishing are knots that are overhand and barrel knot.

The folding techniques are also reliable finishing methods. For materials that are flexible, such as cotton, the only thing you have be able to accomplish is lay the cords in a flat position against the back surface and apply glue to the ends to keep them in the desired position. For materials that are less flexible you can fold the cords towards the back, slide them through a loop made from some knots. then apply glue, let it dry and then remove any the excess material.

Then, you can finish your finishing using the help of fringes. You can pick between a brushed or beaded fringe.

Connecting Cords

When working on Macrame projects you will always be confronted with the task of adding cords on top of an existing one, or any other surface, such as dowels or rings. The process of attaching cords onto surfaces typically known as mounting. The most commonly used method to employ is to use the Reverse Larks Head Knot , which is used to connect additional cords to a dowel or ring. dowel. When adding cords to existing cords the new cords need to be incorporated into the design overall. To avoid the pattern's lopsidedness it is essential to include an equal number of cords for both sides in certain projects. It is also important to eliminate gaps when you add new cords. The possibility of adding new cords onto an existing cord by using this knot: the square, linked knot overhand knot, or the standard knot overhand. Other methods for adding cords are the diamond stitch as well as triangular knots.It is possible to add cords using the triangle knot.

# Chapter 10: Macrame Jewellery

Macrame jewelry is all the rage whether vintage, boho or hippie, If you're walking around with your own macrame jewelry, an eye-catching anklet or striking brooch, you'll not just be noticed in summer but also in. Macrame jewelry is a symbol of simplicity, naturalness, and unadulterated appeal, which is why it is especially popular among young women and those with a youthful spirit. However, not just the women of the world appreciate macrame jewellery More and more guys are also sporting their own macrame anklets or bracelets as a sign of their individual style. Are you looking to create your first macrame piece or are you already a pro at macrame and seeking new ideas and inspiration for macrame jewelry? If so, you'll discover something new with us. In our shop , you'll not only find everything about macrame but you will also find a wealth of tips and tricks to help you out.

Make macrame jewelry yourself

Macrame is a remarkably ancient knotting technique created in the Orient hundreds of years ago. It has gained popularity across the globe over time. Macrame accessories and jewelry are also manufactured by hand in China, Peru or in Northern Europe. The unique thing about this is that anyone with the appropriate technology to create macrame jewelry can make new masterpieces repeatedly. By using other substances, one can design unlimited variations. For instance, you could make macrame jewelry for a variety of occasions, from elegant stylish and classy to distinctive and fun for festivals in the summer. It's not just the basic technology and the versatility which make macrame jewellery so popular. The natural style created by macrame jewelry and other items. make the handmade jewelry popular even with those who are usually not interested in jewelry.

Material to make a macrame necklace

If you're planning to make macrame bracelets or a macrame anklet it is necessary to have a variety of materials. The most crucial element is the macrame thread that is the base for this macrame wristband. Based on the way your personal piece of jewelry should appear like, additional items and even some accessories are needed. The following items are recommended:

* Safety pin

* scissors

* Tape measures

* Glue

* Clasp

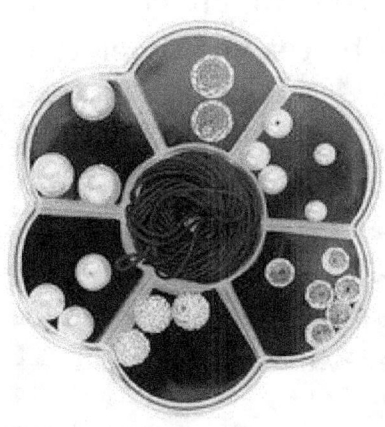

The needle is used to create the macrame bracelet, which is fastened when you are weaving. This is ideal when it is placed with a pillow is sitting on your lap. Cut the macrame thread. A tape measure can help you determine the right length before. Glue on the other hand is a great option to secure knots in the middle and near the conclusion on your macrame wristband. However, make sure that the glue you use is clear and quick drying. Also, you should make sure to use it as minimally as you can so that the appearance of the macrame jewellery does not get damaged. It is possible to attach a clasp to the macrame bracelet in order to enable the secure locking system. You can also use a clasp without a clasp and join the bracelet using knots.

Macrame jewelry: which yarn to use? What yarn is best suited to be used in macrame jewellery?

Traditional macrame yarns that are made from sisal, jute or hemp aren't suitable for production of high-end macrame jewellery. The reason for this is that the natural fibers that are not treated are rough and people find too rough. Macrame yarns constructed from these materials are far too heavy to be used to make a fine macrame bracelet. Instead, a thinner cotton thread or embroidery floss is suggested. It is possible to divide it into different threads, to allow you to, for instance, create friendship bracelets with macrame designs. Are you interested in making it even simpler for you? In our store, you can find the appropriate yarn to make macrame jewellery on purchase.

Decorating Macrame Jewellery

Macrame jewelry made by hand is especially evident because it is decorated with various kinds of materials. If you make your bracelet with a macrame design it is possible to include additional items at the beginning. Glass beads, wood beads, or plastic beads are equally appropriate as rocailles beads, semi-precious stones or freshwater pearls. Sequins, pendants and bells are also employed in a macrame necklace or macrame jewelry to be made into. What you want to wear is acceptable.

Tip: Do love genuine jewelry pieces and that's the reason you're so keen on macrame jewelry? Are you looking for unique necklaces and charms that you are associated with memories? An old shell from your holiday at the beach or a pendant with an initial or a stone set into the shell - the list of options is endless.

Making a macrame-inspired bracelet How can you create an individual macrame bracelet?

Whatever you decide to do, whether you'd like to create a macrame bracelet or macrame hair accessory, macrame jewelry, a macrame brooch, or other macrame accessories yourself, you must follow the correct instructions. The simple act of tying threads in a random manner does not produce a great outcome. It is possible to purchase various macrame books through us, with a wealth of information on how to make a macrame jewelry stand. It is essential to always tie your knots tight or loosely. Particularly for filigree macrames it is recommended to secure them. This will make the bracelet stronger and more durable. A simple knot technique can be enough to create a variety of macrame bracelets. Here's a brief instruction:

Step 1 Make four ribbons each one approx. one meter long at the highest point.

Step 2: Wrap the right band into an elongated loop that is left of the middle band and slide it under that band to the left's outside.

Step 3. Slide the left band in front of the middle band and then pull it forward into the loop created by the right band.

Step 4: Gently draw the edges of your left and right straps until the knot is formed.

A tip: This straightforward method to tie a macrame wristband is already a possibility to alter by using two different methods Make the loop in the second step by always using the ribbon to the right side, and you will get macrame bracelets that are three-dimensionally curving like the spiral. If you change the right and left sides to create a smooth or even a macrame-like bracelet.

# Chapter 11: How To Make A Bracelet

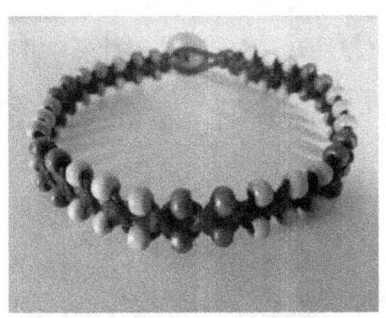

The Double Beaded Macrame Bracelet

Materials List

Black cord that is waxed

- 40cm of 2mm thick black waxed Cord

60 - beads of 4-6mm (hole is at minimum 1mm wide)

Flat button or bead (hole must be at the center as well as at least 2mm in width)

* PVA glue

* Nail varnish that is clear

Tools List

* Pins and Macrame boards (optional)

* A craft knife sharp-pointed scissors

Step 1: The ends of 1mm cable in polish that is clear. If you are using super glue, apply a drop of it to each end. Let it dry. This prevents the cord's ends from fraying, and makes it easier to thread the beads for the next steps.

Make sure you tie and loop the middle of the cord large enough that the beads can pass through by applying some force. If the fit is not tight enough, the bracelet could fall off. The loop should be secured to the macrame board when you are using.

Step 2. Fold the wrapped cord into half. This is the way to tie knots. The cord should be placed under the length of the board. Tie a square knot on the length of the cord and the shorter end is left making the loop.

Make sure the knot is tight.

Step 3: Attach one bead to either end of cord. Then, push them upwards until they rest against the cord's central point.

Step 4: Make a knot of a square beneath the beads. As you tie the knot, adjust the tension of the thread and beads to ensure that the beads are in contact with the cord's central point.

Step 5 Repeat the steps 4, 5 and 6 until you've thirty pairs.

Step 6: Cut off the remaining knotting cords, and then cover the ends as well as the area around them with PVA glue. Don't worry about the glue sticking out since it'll dry completely. Let the glue dry until it's at the very least, dry.

7. Thread your button, or the flat beads on to the central cord , and with a little space to allow movement, tie a knot to secure it to the cord. Take off the remainder of the central cord, leaving a shorter end. The end of the cord can be coated with the clear varnish in order to keep it from fraying, or left in its natural state.

Apple Macrame Endless Fall Bracelet

Materials List

* 60cm length of cotton cord with black waxed wax

* 40-inch length of red cotton cord with waxed finish

* 1 8-10mm flat bead

Tools List

* Pins and Macrame board (optional)

* Scissors

* Ruler

* PVA glue

Step 1: Divide the cord into two. lay it out in front your side or attach it onto the macrame boards.

Step 2. The red cord is folded in half and put the half-way point under those black cords.

Step 3: The red cords are crossed across the front of the black. It doesn't matter which cord is placed on the top. Just make sure that it's the same for every knot else the pattern won't form properly.

Step 4: Pick up the black cords and run their way through the loop created from the two red cords, and through the black cords.

Step 5 - Secure it by pulling black cord towards the downwards.

The knot should be placed approximately 1 cm below the black cord's end and create the loop. The loop is part of the bracelet's fastener and should be fitted tightly so that the bead can be able to pass through.

Step 6 Step 6 - Connect the red cords to the the cords in black.

Step 7: Pick up the black cords, and thread their way through the loop made through the cords of red, and through the black cords.

Step 8 8. The black cords should be pulled downwards , tightening the knot until it is under the knot you made the first time.

Step 9 Repetition steps 6-8, until your bracelet is 7.5 inches in length. By holding all four cords to the cross-over point using one hand, and then making sure to thread the black cords through the other hand is a great method for making this type knot.

Step 10 - Tie one square knot with the red cords, and make sure the knot is tight.

Step 11 - Cut off any excess red cords as well as one length from black cord.

Step 12 : Cover cord's ends and the surrounding area with PVA glue. Allow to dry.

Step 13 - Attach the flat bead to the black cord. With a gap of 3mm, make an overhand knot hold the bead.

Step 14 Cut off the remainder of the cord, leaving a shorter end. The cord's ends could be coated with PVA in order to stop its fraying.

Zig Zag Bracelet

Materials List

* 60cm of length of 2mm black cotton cord that has been waxed

* 150cm length of cotton cord in black waxed cotton

The beads are oval in size. (must have a hole of 2mm at a minimum)

* 1 15mm disc bead or button with a central hole (minimum hole diameter of 4mm) Tools List

* Macrame board and pins (optional)

* Scissors

• Clear nail varnish (optional)

* PVA glue

Step 1: Cut the length that is shorter the cord into half. Then put it around the pin of your macrame board depending on. If not, simply place the cord on an even surface.

Step 2. Fold the longer cord length in half. Then tie a square knot over the shorter cords.

This knot should be positioned in a way that the loop formed at the end of the cords with shorter lengths is snug enough so that the disk beads be able to pass through.

Step 3. Tie another three square knots.

Step 4: Thread eight beads through the central cords.

Step 5 - Take the longer cord to the right side and carry this across your central cord beneath the initial bead then under the central cords , so that it comes out again on the right side beneath the first bead of the right side of the central cord.

Step 6 Repeat step 5 until you've put the right cord on each of the beads, shifting the beads around as you move them.

Step 7: Hold the right cord on the lower end of the beads, repeat steps 5 and 6 with the left-side longer cord.

Step 8: Then tie a round knot in order to secure cords.

Step 9 : Tie the remaining four square knots that coincide with the knots at beginning of the bracelet.

10. Cut off any excess lengths of outer cord and secure the ends as well as the surrounding region by gluing them with PVA. The glue is used to secure the ends, and it will dry transparent, so it will not appear. The glue should dry.

Attach the disk bead to the two cords that are central and, leave a space of few millimetres. Tie the knot overhand to hold it in place. When you have cut off any cord that is left in step 11, the ends of the cord can be dipped in clear nail varnish, if you want to. After drying, this will prevent cutting the cord.

# Chapter 12: How To Create Common Macrame Knots And Patterns

Patterns, knots and macrame knots are easy and cost-effective learning tools. They require only a few resources and an knowledge of the knots. This chapter will provide you with six common macrame knots that you can utilize to build a variety of macrame-related projects.

Here are a few terms that you must know prior to starting:

Knotting thread

The cord or collection that creates the knot needed for a specific step.

Knot the string

The cord is the loop that is wrapped around the wires.

Sennit.

This is a grouping from the identical thread that is often used to work out. For instance when you make 6 half knots within one row, you'll have 6 half knots the sennit.

Reverse Larkshead Knot

It is the Reverse Larkshead Knot is the standard method to put your macrame cords on the top of your project.

Make half a string of Macrame. Attach the loop to the cords of the dowel.

Take the string off the dowel. Then pull the cords and create pretzel.

Pull the two cords in a knot to secure the knot on the top.

A Half knot

This video demonstrates the four-corded Half Knot. The exterior strings are all knotting strings. The 2 middle strings serve as knotting strings. In addition to the knotting cords place the left knotting cable to the right , and that knotting cord to the left.

The knotting string should be placed to the left of the two knotting strings. Then, put that knotting string is to your left. Pull the half knot of the lock.

If you make with a half knot naturally spiral

Square Knot

The Knot Square will fit the Knot Square, and the first part of the knot is an oblique knot. the square is then completed using the opposite cords, with an effective half knot. Step by step examine the whole knot in the square:

The first four steps above are exactly the same similar to the steps of half knots. Then , we'll reverse the process: cross through two knotted cords, and finally the right knotting line to the left side under one knotting string. The left side is left.

The right knotting string should be placed under the knotting strings, and then over the knotting line to the right. Make sure you tie the knot in a safe square.

Half Hitch Knot

There are a variety of variations to the Half Hitch Knot. This is an Half-Hitch Vertical that has two strings serving as knotting cords on the left side and an edging cord to the left. It is sometimes known as "left over right."

Put your left hand (knotting) across the left line (knotting).

Tie the knotting cord in the direction of the knotting cord to make a loop, then insert it over and into the cord that is knotted.

Pull the sturdy Half Brace.

Repeat the process for an stitch. Naturally, a half-hitch knot will spiral:

The above directions indicate the fact that Half Hitch only operated vertically using two cords. It is possible to use a variety of wire and cord knotting. On a horizontal hook, you can have between six and eight knotting cords, with a rope suspended over it.

Diagonal Half Stitch

A Diagonal Half-Hitch can be pinned diagonally to the point until it is worked. These are the instructions:

Make sure you secure the cords of your dowel. A reverse-lateral knot is a way to save these cords. Left cords are the knot-bearing one in our instance, along with all other cords that are knotting cords.

Place a pin just to the left of the cord that is knotted to ensure the knot is secure.

The knot-bearing thread should be placed across the knotting lines on an angle. Then, click on the cords towards the right.

Start with the initial (more left) cord knotting. Then, thread it under and over the cord of knot.

Use the same knotting string. It is then looped through the knot-bearing rope, then through the loop that is between it and the knot that was tied earlier. Shoot safely

Continue to follow the two previous steps starting from the left, knotting every knotted rope until the diagonal end is reached.

Horizontal halving is possible using the knot-bearing rope similarly, but only horizontally.

It's a three-square knot or triangular knot and it is a single Sennit.

Overhand Knot

Modern braiding techniques in the Macrame is possible to add. However, the base of the braid must be covered using macrame knots in order to stop the braids from becoming lost.

This is a basic braiding guideline (equal to braiding hair) which is secured using Five vertical Half Hitch Knots, and finally overhand Knot. It is the Overhand Knot is like the Half Hitch except that it is worked with an unlooped cord (rather than a loop attached to another knot-bearing cord).

The braid is made using twin cords to each of the 3 pieces. Set 1 2, Set 2 3, Set 3 Numbered to the left.

Halfway Knot Braid

Set 1 over Set 2. Set 1. Bring Set 3 to Set 1.

Set 2. Over Set 3. Set 2.

Set 1. Place 1. Set on 3.

Set 2 was placed onto Set 1.

Make the same pattern again if wish to make it braid.

The thread that knots will be that left-hand loop. The rest of the cords are knot-bearing. Put the left cord on top of the right one in the vertical loop (see above). It should be obvious how it appears like:

By a single vertical hitch, the braid is fixed, but a 5 , or 6 hitch is more frequent.

Use an overhand knot to completely ensure the stitch is protected. Make the loop of the knot using the knotting cord that is on the other side of your braid.

Make sure the knot is secured.

# Chapter 13: Macrame Projects

Mason Jar Wall Hanging

In the realm of tools for art, Mason jars have remained very popular. They can be useful for everything from canning to sorting many other applications that are innovative. It is possible to use any jar to create a fresh elegant, neat, and distinctive decoration to your home using this macrame-based mason jar hanger for plants. It looks great at a gathering or by itself and make the new apartment or home the perfect housewarming gift. Create your macrame hanging device as large or tiny as you'd like , and then hang it in a bright spot to ensure that your plant is growing and secure in your mason jar.

Materials:

1. A mason jars

2. A pair of scissors

3. Macrame cords

4. A plant

5. Soil to feed the plant

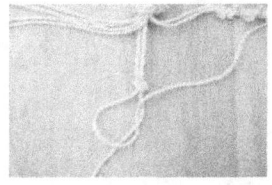

It is necessary to use mason jars for this project. Make sure it can hold plants that require a bit of room to grow. A pint-sized or bigger will certainly be a good starting place. Pick the best form of macrame cord which can range from cotton to polyester to jute. It all depends on the style you like and the strength you'd like your cord.

Steps:

1. Knot and cut

Cut four lengths of cords, each about three yards in length. Then fold them in half, and then at the halfway mark, tie them all together, creating an elongated loop around the knot. This is the place where you'll hang your final piece on the ceiling or wall.

2. Create pairs

The cords are split into two pairs consisting of two cords. Make sure you leave about four to five inches distance from the top of the knot , and connect the two cords.

3. You can tie the knots in a spiral fashion.

Create the spiral knot underneath the knots of each set. Choose a pair, and make sure the right cord is taut. Transfer the left cord to the right side, and then back and upwards, through the loop created. Then pull it tight. Repeat this process with the same cord keeping the first right cord taut. Eventually, an elongated spiral knot will begin to emerge. Continue to weave the loops of the knots till they reach about four inches.

4. The knots should be longer.

After all your strings are knotted in a spiral leaving about 12 inches on each cord. You can tie a knot on each string in the direction of 12 inches.

inches.

5. Alternating pairs

Lay out the sets. Pick the right cord from the leftmost set , and connect it to the left cord from the closest set, approximately 3 inches, just below the tie previously tied. Keep going, switching between the two sets. Pick up the two cords that are outside at the end, and connect them.

6. Knot the cords

About 3 inches lower than the knot's range, tie all the cords with a single knot. Hang the string for about 12 inches and then trim the ends.

7. Plant the plant

Set up a mason jar by in it, and fill it with soil and the plants you prefer. It may be best to plant the plant prior to deciding on the dimensions of your plant, then place the mason jar inside Macrame's hanger.

8. Enjoy the moment and hang out!

9. It's hard to see why you shouldn't make at least four of these adorable miniature

planters to liven up your office, space or kitchen!

Macrame Plant Hanger Beginner

Description: Plant hanger measuring 2.25 feet 5.5 inches (75 cm) Knots are: square knot and alternating square knots half knot and gathering knot.

62

Supplies:

Cord Ten strands of cord that measure 18 feet 0.5 inches (5,5 meters) 2 cords of 3 feet and 3.3 inches (1 meter)

Ring 1 circular rings (wood) that measures 1.6 millimeters (4 centimeters) diameter

Container: 7.25 inches (18 cm) diameter

Instructions (step-by-step):

1. The 10 long cords in half , passing them through the wooden rings.

2. Join each of the (now 20) cords together by tying one shorter strand by tying an

edging knot. Put the cords that have been cut away in a drawer after knotting the knot for gathering.

3. Create a square knot by using all cords: take four strands from each side to create the square knot. The remaining 12 strands are at the center.

4. Divide the strands into two sets of 10 Strands each. Secure a square knot on each set, using three strands each (4 Strands remain within the middle of the set).

5. The strands are divided into three sets of 6 strands to form the outer groups, and 8 strands to form the group within the middle. Make a square knot inside each set by using two strands per side.

63

6. Split the strands into five sets of 4 strands and tie an equilateral knot for each set.

7. Continue to the 5 sets. In the outer two sets there are four square knots to tie. Then, in the three inner sets there are 9 knots in half.

8. Utilizing all sets tie 7 square knots alternately by joining two strands of each set by connecting the left two strands in the set. In the first three, fourth, fifth and seventh rows you're not using the outer strands of each side.

9. Repeat steps 7 and 8. In the next step, you tie 5 square knots alternating instead of 7 square knots in alternating rows.

64

10. To assist you in the steps, you can number all the threads left-to-right, and then number them no.1 up to. 20.

11. With the four middle braids (no. 9-12) you create fourteen square knots.

12. Create a square knot using your set of four braids n. 3 to 6, and the set of four

Strands No. 15-18.

13. Divide the strands into four sets of four Strands (ignore the set with 14 strands).

Square knots in between) as well as tie twelve square knots into each set.

14. Drop two inches (5 cm).

15. Create five sets following the following method and tie each set with a square knot:. Set 1 is made up of strands number. 5, 6, 1, and 2

b. Set 2 is made up of strands number. 3, 4, 9, and 10

C. Set 3 is comprised of strands nos. 7 7, 13, and 14

D. Set 4 is made up of strands number. 11 12, 17 and 18

E. Set 5 is made up of strands number. 19 20 and 15

16. Add an additional 2 inches (5 cm) without knots. This is the time to set your bowl or container on the hanger to be sure that it is able to fit. If you have to leave more space and not knots to accommodate your container, you may do that.

17. All strands should be joined and tie a knot to gather them together using the shorter strand left. The strands should be cut to various lengths to finish the project.

Macrame Plant Hanger Intermediate

Description: Plant hanger measuring 4,3 inches and 4 inches (1,30 meter) The number 67

Knots: Square knot, alternating square knot, half knot, alternating half hitch, gathering knot.

Supplies:

- - Cords: eight strands that measure 26ft and (8 meters) 1 shorter cord

- Wooden Ring 1 circle band (wood) with a 1,6 inch (4 centimeters) diameter

Container/Flowerpot 7.25 inches (18 centimeters) in diameter. Instructions (step-by-step):

1. The cord is folded in half (the long ones) in half, then through the rings.

You now have 16 cords total. Set them up in sets of four cords.

2. Attach four square knots to the four sets of strands.

3. The drop is 3.15 inches (8 cm).

4. Make sure you tie four strands of each set and tie the left pair of set next to it. Repeat this on all four sets.

5. The drop is 4.3 inches (11 centimeters).

6. Repeat step 4 starting with the two right strands , this time.

7. Make 2 strands of one set and tie 10 half-hitch knots. Repeat the same process for the left and right strands from that set. Repeat for all sets.

69

8. Take a step back 3.9 inches (10 cm) and make a row of 48 half knots to the four sets of strands.

9. Choose the two middle strands from each set and tie 8 half-hitch knots in alternating order. Leave the two strands to the side of the set in their natural state (without knots).

10. Create 30 half knots along every set of 4 strands.

11. Make use of a new cord to tie an encircling knot that wraps around the entire strand.

12. Cut off the ends and then fray them in the manner you like.

## 70

## Macrame Plant Hanger Advanced

Description: A plant hanger measuring 2.25 feet 5.5 inches (75 cm) Knots include: square knot, alternating circle knot gathering knot , and overhand knot.

Supplies:

* Cord four strands from 13 feet 1.5 inches (4 meters) four cords that measure 16 feet 4.8 inches (5 meters) 2 cords of 3 feet and 3.4 inches (1 meter)

* Ring 1. A round rings (wood) that measures 1.5 millimeters (4 centimeters) diameter

* Beads: wooden beads

* Cristal Bowl/Container 7 " (18 centimeters) in diameter. directions (step-by-step):

## 71

1. The 8 long cords (4 cords that measure 13 feet 1.5 inches ) into four

Strands of 16 feet and 4.8 inches) cut in half using the wooden rings.

2. Join the entire (now 16) cords together, and tie one shorter strand by tying an edging knot. Put the cords that have been cut away in a drawer after you tie the knot for gathering.

## 72

3. Split the lengths of the strands in four sets of four strands per. Each set contains two long strands as well as two shorter lengths. Make five Chinese crown knots into each set. Make sure that each strand is tight and smooth.

4. Make 8 knots of squares on every set with four strings. In each set, the two shorter strands are located in the middle, and you are tied with the two larger strands on the outer edges.

5. Ties 15 half square knots each set.

73

6. Take a step back 5.5 inches (14 cm) with no knots and tie an alternate square knot to join the two cords left in each set.

7. Take a drop of 3.15 inches (8 cm) and tie in a square knot that alternates with four strands.

8. Then drop down 1.5 inches (4 cm). Place the bowl or container you want to use in the hanger to make sure it is able to fit. connect all strands and then tie a knot of gathering with the strand left over. Add a small bead to each strand , 74

End (optional). Make an overhand knot on the strands and trim all strands to just below the knots.

Hanger For Wooden Dowel

75

Make a macrame cord which measures three feet (1 meters) and attached to a dowel made of wood. Join the two ends of the dowel with one end. It is going to be used this to hang your macrame project after it's finished. At first I prefer to hang it to my wall, so that I can hang up my macrame work as I tie knots. It's much easier to do this as opposed to determining it.

Cut your macrame rope in 12 lengths of string that are 15 foot (4.5 metres) long with a cutters. It may appear like a large amount of cord, however knots make longer than you would think. If you're in need of it and you don't have the means to increase the thickness of the rope and you'll need to cut it more than you would.

Make one of the macrame cores into two on the dowel made of wood and tie it with an adle's head knot to secure it to a dowel made of wood.

76

Join the other cords the same manner

Then, take the four strings, and then make a left-facing spiral stitch (also called half knot Lynton) by knotting thirteen half knots.

Four ropes are used to make an additional spiral stitch consisting of 13 half knots, using the same four ropes. Continue working using four-chord. There should be minimum six spiral stitches by the time you're done.

77

Make sure you are about 2 inches from the knot that you tied in a spiral. This is where the knot known as the square knot is located.

Create a right knot profile using all four string. Continue to create the right knots all through this row. Try to ensure they are all evenly vertically. You'll end having six knots.

A second row of square knots is the best time to begin the square knots so that we can tie knots in a "V" shape.

Start by opening the first two strings , and the two strings that are left. Think about each of the four square knots facing right. There is now another line that includes the first two knots, and the last two cords that are not knotted as well as five knots. It does not matter how you place them, just make sure you make sure to keep them close.

Continue to decrease the square knots "V" made from the square knots on the third row. The first four strings , and the final four strings are left out. There will be four knots. The fourth row, towards the highest point, you'll leave six cords, and at the bottom six cords. There will be 3 square tie-ups. On the 5th row at the beginning, you'll find eight cords, and at the end, you'll have eight cords. Then you'll have two square tie. In the sixth and last row, tie ten cords to 78

The beginning and the ten cords at the end need ready to release. You can tie a square knot using four strings.

Square Knots Square making another "V in square knots This time we'll expand the knots into a triangle, or upside down" V "For this first section take in the eight first and the last eight cords. It will result in 2 square knots.

79

You've probably heard of macrame, whether you grew up in the 70s or have been browsing on Pinterest for some time. Macrame patterns are elaborate that include a range of knots that come in a variety of dimensions and shapes.

A few of the most well-known examples you can find on the internet are wall decors However, using this technique and materials, you could achieve much more. We're still waiting for some of these amazing projects, we've made the decision to shift the attention off of the walls towards more practical designs.

These tutorials using macrame are great for those who are new to the subject Some of them are completed with the use of a single Node. The demonstrations do not have nodes but makes use of macrame cords to spin instead. Are you interested in learning more? Check out the following examples.

But first, you need to learn to create some basic macrame knots prior to launching one of the projects listed below. Learn these knots until you're confident about the final result as much as you can.

A Macrame Table Runner

A Beautiful Mess The majority of macrame table runners are on the market We love the one from the beautiful Mess. The pictures break the pattern down into easy steps, and then the 80

Instructions are easy to follow. It's interesting to learn the best way to tie the knot without record, however these photos will give you a clear picture of how each knot looks like.

I am talking in layers of coordination and contrasts while decorating each space.

These three elements make a room more complicated regardless of whether it's color, texture or scale. The fourth rule of thumb is polyvalence! This table runner made sure to check every box and created the small space with its minimalist and fascinating design more distinctive.

All you have to know are the three most important nodes and you'll are left with a beautiful layer that can be used throughout the year. If you are familiar with the knots we've taught you and you are able to tailor your table runner to match the size of the table, or modify it completely and make an elongated macrame wall.

## Conclusion

Because of the creative nature of macrame's knottingprocess, lots people love doing it as a hobby. Actually, some believe macrame can be a natural treatment to boost mental capabilities to strengthen joints and arms as well as improve concentration and quiet the mind. However, this does not mean that exceptional artistic talent is required. It is essential to master macrame at peace and then carefully make knots of leather and cords.

Macrame is also used in a variety of fashion and home products. Shoes, bags, clothing and jewelry, door hangers plant hangers and hanging baskets can be embellished with this traditional braiding.

In bracelets macrame is beautiful and makes your appearance. It also speaks volumes regarding your selection of fashion accessories, given the generally believed that jewelry made by hand is typically meticulously made. Typically, this type of rope braiding technique is employed to keep gems and beads together securely and elegantly. It's also flexible as it is adjustable and adaptable to various kinds of.

The variety of macrame is what makes it the ideal combination for gemstones with vibrant colors and other beads that make bracelets enchanting.

The most crucial rule of Macrame is "Practice improves". If you don't practice regularly your skills are bound to decline with time. Keep the skills you have developed, train your creative part within your head, as well as continue making amazing handmade creations. Jewelry and fashion accessories created using even the simplest Macrame knots will always be stunning to beholdand are perfect for gifts to family members on special occasions. Gifting a Macrame ring to one of your loved ones, for instance, conveys your message of love and appreciation that you didn't forget to give them a present, but that you cherish the person so much that you have put your effort in creating something unique for them. And it is an extremely effective message. The most appealing aspect of Macrame is its ability to make durable objects. This means that you can keep an ornamental piece or an accessory that you designed for yourself over the years while enjoying the value, and be able to feel nostalgic every time you recall the moment you made it. It's even better when you created it together with someone. This durability feature makes Macrame products incredibly great presents.

Macrame is also an avenue to start your own small-scale enterprise. Once you have mastered your Macrame abilities, you will be able to easily sell your products and receive a good price for your items, particularly in the event that you can create products like bracelets that consumers purchase a lot of. You can even teach people to start your own business that creates customized Macrame fashion accessories. The possibilities Macrame has are limitless.

Keep in mind that each knot will be the base of different projects you will create So you're going to need take time to master every one of them. Then, work on them until they're the way you want to be. It is unlikely that you will achieve them flawlessly immediately, so be patient and ensure that you master the right thing before moving into the next.

Don't worry if aren't able to master it at first, it's going to get better over time, and the more effort you invest in it, the more proficient you will develop. It takes some time and effort to master it however, the more effort and time you invest in it, the more successful you will become. My aim with this tutorial is to provide you with the motivation and direction that you require to master macrame.

It's not easy initially however the more effort you do the more simple it's getting until it's effortless to you. I'm sure you'll be able to be in love with every aspect of this passion once you understand how to weave knots, you'll want to create them in every way you are able to.

Don't be concerned about the color and don't be concerned about not getting it perfect at first. This will provide you all the information you require to get it done exactly how you want it to. And it will show you that you can achieve everything when you work on macrame projects.

I'm hoping that you will get better at this craft and make the projects you'd like by using the patterns you select. There is no limit to the possibilities of creating macrame designs, and the more comfortable you are in them the more simple it will be to design your own macrame projects no matter what you'd like them to look like. So, get into macrame both feet, and you will discover that nothing can stop you from achieving your goals with these projects.

What do you have to be doing you The only thing it will require is energy and time, and you're getting exactly what you want from your macrame-related projects. From now on, you're getting closer to becoming the master of macrame and you will become awestruck by all things macrame. Macrame's world is waiting for you and is asking you to take a dive and start learning.

Good luck and be creative until your heart's content.

Stay sharp continue to practice and keep working to improve. You are now in the realm that is endlessly exciting!

Stop reading, start doing!

www.ingramcontent.com/pod-product-compliance
Lightning Source LLC
Chambersburg PA
CBHW071841080526
44589CB00012B/1078